SHAHRYAR SADREE

DOWN
in a
HOLE

A Handbook for Life Mastery

INKS & BINDINGS

Inks and Bindings
888-290-5218
www.inksandbindings.com
orders@inksandbindings.com

Images in this book were selected for educational purposes only. Some were taken by the author or donated to the author. All other images in this book are in the public domain No copyright infringement is intended.

Page 20 – Centralia, Pennsylvania – Photo taken by author

Page 87 – Selection on the ramp at Auschwitz-Birkenau, 1944 (Auschwitz Album) 1c.jpg

https://commons.wikimedia.org/wiki/File:Selection_on_the_ramp_at_Auschwitz-Birkenau,_1944_(Auschwitz_Album)_1c.jpg

Date: May or June 1944, Auschwitz-Birkenau, Poland

Source: Yad Vashem. The album was donated to Yad Vashem by Lili Jacob (later Lili Jacob-Zelmanovic Meier, a survivor, who found it in the Mittelbau-Dora concentration camp in 1945.

Author: Unknown. Several sources believe the photographer to have been Ernst Hoffmann or Bernhard Walter of the SS.

Page 88 – Birkenau a group of Jews walking towards the gas chambers and crematoria.jpg

https://commons.wikimedia.org/wiki/File:Birkenau_a_group_of_Jews_walking_towards_the_gas_chambers_and_crematoria.jpg

Date: 27 May 1944

Source: Auschwitz Album ([https://collections.ushmm.org/search/catalog/pa8538 record in USHMM collection).

Author: anonymous, possibly SS photographers E. Hoffmann & B. Walter.

Pages 92 & 93 – Duck and Cover

https://www.loc.gov/item/mbrs01836081/

United States Office Of Civil Defense, and Archer Productions. Duck and Cover. 1951. Video. https://www.loc.gov/item/mbrs01836081/.

Page 95 – Mother and masked children exiting a grocery store

Author: Shahryar Sadree

Actors: Ashly Holiday with her boys, Jasper and Gunnar Benson.

Page 96 – Child wearing a cloth mask

Author: Leo Fontes

Actor: Eliana Buenas

Parents: Steven & Dara Buenas

Page 109 – Censored Image

Illustration created by the author.

Contents

PREFACE

There are times when we feel like we are beaten and life has taken away our will to go on. Moments like these are not uncommon, even for the strongest of people. We all have a moment of weakness, and even those that seem to have it all, eventually find themselves in a hole at some point in their lives. Being a strong-willed person does not make one immune from being human. As much as we try to hide our imperfections from the rest of the world, we cannot hide them from ourselves. For we know who we are inside... or do we?

The feelings of helplessness can easily overwhelm us, if we allow it space to root in our minds. Many of us have accepted the four walls of our minds as the way things are going to be. Only a few will take a sledge hammer to those walls and claim the life they want to experience. In this book, you will find that being ***down in a hole*** is not the end to your life, but only another fork in the road. Life is all about choices, and choices are a powerful force of nature. If we learn how to master the power of choice, we will have learned how to master our lives. Our lives are what they are because we have chosen to *experience* it the way we do. The world is what it is today because we created it with the choices we have made.

A Bigger Picture
Every one of us has partaken in the creation process of everything we see wrong and right in our world today. I have included many examples that are eye-opening. Whether we have contributed consciously or unconsciously, there is no doubt that it took every single human on the planet to create our world and all of its imperfections. When we can accept our part, then we can correct it. It isn't until the moment that we take ownership of our faults that things begin to make sense to us. Only then are we to find a way out of the hole we are in. Every morning we get up to face another day, we have been given another gift. This is why it's called the present.

Today is a present. Today is another chance to right what we see as being wrong. We can only make the changes within ourselves, but by doing so, we *actually* change the world. Our creation then becomes more like the one we picture in our minds.

Create the Life You Want

We have so much power within us to create the lives we want to experience, but many of us have given up on ourselves because of things we have experienced in the *past*. This is something we must overcome if we want to get out of our hole. Another liability we must conquer is our own system of beliefs. In order to keep an open mind, our current beliefs must be shattered. Our most useful tool here is the power of an open mind. The mind works a lot like a parachute in this respect; it works best when it is open.

Beliefs are very powerful, so we need to learn how and when to use them. It is very important to be aware of what is going on around us. To win, we must be ready to accept what is, and adapt to the environment. This means we must be willing to change, because change is going to occur anyway and it does not require our acceptance or approval. Mastering the rules of life means to be aware of them, and how your actions affect everything after them. You will win more when you learn the rules to any game. Life's rules are simple if you pay attention to the details. Nothing in life is free. You will pay something at some point. The least you will pay is *attention*!

No one is immune to the pitfalls of life. There are always going to be ups and downs, but that is what makes life so interesting. Without the lows, we would never know the highs. Finding yourself **down in a hole** is an opportunity to discover the power within you to create another high...on *demand*. We are talking about life *mastery* here! This little book contains enough knowledge to begin your journey. In time you will find that life is not as complicated as we make it in our minds. The problem is not that we do not have the tools to dig our way out. It seems more like some have no desire to leave their hole, and some have given up on trying anymore. Defeat is hard to overcome. But if we cannot move past defeat, or any of our other mental blockers, we will become a prisoner to our own ego. *Life mastery begins and ends with self.* The outside world has no jurisdiction to the inside. But the inside world has much influence on the outside world. Both are inter-connected and the outside world can also affect the inside, and usually does. Not because the outside world's dominance, but rather the *values* we place on each event that occurs on the outside. All these calculations are made in a matter of seconds. And all these programmed responses are triggered by a value system of beliefs that is stored on a virtual hard drive that we call **the mind.**

Aren't the Mind and Brain the Same?

Short answer: *Uh, no.* **Explanation:** the brain is more like the hardware. It is a part of the physical body. We use the brain to 100% of its capacity. The mind is something completely different. Mind is like the software. An operating system, navigation system and an unlimited storage-space virtual hard drive all-in-one! We have been able to learn enough about it to use only a small fraction of its *full* potential.

Mind is non-physical. It is something completely misunderstood and misrepresented. I firmly believe it is because we have lost touch with what it means to be human so much so, that we have forgotten who and what we are. As we let our mind run free on auto-pilot, the world we create *blindly* is rapidly spinning out of control, and now, it is consuming us. It's time to wake up and take ownership of everything that's ours.

Author's Message to the Reader:

This book started as random inspired thoughts. As time went on, the pieces fit like a puzzle. Piece by piece, as I started to see the picture reveling itself to me, I started to wonder if there was a reason why so much useful information was kept hidden so well right in front of our eyes? In that moment I knew the impact my work will have on those who pick it up and read it.

When you discover the delicate nature of the human mind, and security vulnerabilities you are open to by *not* being aware of the environment you are playing in... everything will begin to make sense. As you read deeper into this book, be prepared to be amazed and horrified all at once!

"You have More Power Than You Will Ever Know."

ACKNOWLEDGEMENTS

Portions of this book were written by: **Maziar Sadree**

I want to dedicate this work to my best friend, **Angie Sadree**. *I couldn't do any of this without your undying love and support. Your strength, loyalty, and kindness are what shaped me into the man I am today. I am forever grateful to have you in my life!*

Special Thanks To:

Mom & Dad Sadree; **Mazi Sadree**; **Brian Dainis** (I can't thank you enough); **Patricia Murphy**; **Sabrina, Joseph, Ricky, Robby**, and **Bill Rodriguez** for all of the local family love and support. Lots of love to my friends, **Colleen Anzano**; **Rhonda Crouse**; **Kirsten Wood**; **John, Pat & Paul Midili**; "**Detroit Dave**" **Holmquist**; **Erik "JoJo" Medeiros**; **Joel Demasky**; **Charlie Wiley**; **John Roshio**; **Mike Flannery**; **Ray Avelares**; **Chris Quinn**; **Frank Randazzo**; **Joe Lombari**; **Bobby Templeton**, and all my **Templeton family**; **James & Amy Presta**; and **Daniel Ryan**. *Friends like you are hard to find*. I love you more than you will ever know.

A very special thanks to: **Tony Mead** (*brother, you are a true investigator and Journalist*) keep up the great work! **Shahram Balaghi**, **Tara Fazli**, and my all my family from around the world. **Nichole & Jon Worley**, and of course, **Robert Gray Jr.** *The future is happening NOW!*

My Nephews: **Joseph Rodriguez** – You are the light kid. Never forget that. **Christopher Aceto** – Never give up on yourself, because you can and will win. **Joey Aceto** – When the student becomes ready...the teacher will appear. Pain is always self-induced and optional...just ask your brother.

I love you both as my own. **Ethan Young** and **Raven Aceto** – Love is a simple thing. Try not to complicate it.

ALL MY BAND BROTHERS: **Andy Joyce; Brian Fury; James Steele; David and Ralph Young; Jim Springer** (R.I.P.); **Talon Blaque; Dan Ricanovich; Michael Blair; Stacy King; Tim Coyle;** and **Wayne Johnson.** Thanks for the wonderful memories and great moments making music together.

Steven Lindsay, stay focused and you will win, kid!

To all who bought this book, or just took the time to read it. I hope this information changes your lives as it has mine. We are all one spirit, and to all souls here and there, I love you all!

A Very Special Thanks to:

Leo Fontes, Steven & Dara Buenas for providing the picture of their precious **Eliana!**

Also to:

Billy Benson & Ashly Holiday and **Jasper Benson, Gunnar Benson,** and **Liam Holiday.** I see you all as my family!

SECTION 1

Pitfalls

Chapter 1:
A Common Point of View

I remember a time when every situation in my life seemed hopeless. I would expect the worst, hoping for something a little better. Most of the time, my expectations were met. That's how I lived back then. I was not actually living, but merely surviving.

The memories of my past are kept with me today only to show the progress I have made in such little time. Hopelessness is only a state of *mind* and not a life sentence. We can change the condition at any moment. It's hard to see this when everything in life seems to be pointing downward. Financial situations, love relationships, family conflicts, and other resentments affect us in ways that we feel are beyond our control. Most things are. But we have the ***power*** to overcome fear if we so choose to use it.

In the darkest hour
When it seems the darkest moments of life have reached our toes, thoughts of silver linings and rainbows are going to be the last thing on our mind. It's in these darkest moments where we have the opportunity to use the power within us to rise. Also, the most *growth* takes place in these dark times. If we push through these trying moments of life, the reward will be growth, along with more strength.

Being stuck is not uncommon. In fact, the challenge to find a way through is what builds character. One quality that is admired among all winners is that they don't quit. Giving up isn't even an option in the winner's thought process. They will try and try until they achieve their goal. It is only through perseverance and discipline where winners are made.

Looking up at the ground

We all have moments where we feel tired and weak. This does not mean that we are weak people. Having a weak moment is part of the human experience. It is there to show us that we are human. What we do in that moment will determine the result and shapes our *experience*.

Being **down in a hole** can be viewed as a temporary setback or a catastrophe. Some will even label it as a mental illness that requires a chemical treatment and doctors. I am not a doctor, but I have found myself in a hole from time to time...I still do. However, it has never stopped me from achieving amazing accomplishments. This goes back to the power of *choice*. Although we can't control every event that takes place in our lives, we can *choose* how an event will *affect* us.

Creating our own problems

Most of the problems in our lives are created in our own minds. We are natural-born creators... that's what we do. The creation of everything begins with a single thought. Emotion behind thought puts that thought into motion. Thoughts are very powerful energy forces, and so are emotions. Placing the two together creates one strong force, so you better know what you are doing when you put emotional stock into your thoughts! Thought and emotion together become very powerful energy. Powerful enough to either manifest your desires or take you on a white-knuckle ride through hell!

Most people either do not believe this, or do not understand it, or both. Those who deny the nature of energy and the science behind it, are struck in their own beliefs. By doing so, they deny themselves and their families a better *quality* of life. Science is how the universe works based on things that we know for *certain*. We call them *facts*. A belief is more of an opinion, not having anything to back it other than what we tell ourselves. Our evolution is *natural* by design. Being stuck in a belief ceases the evolutionary process and will place you in a *hole*. Until you figure out the error in *thinking*, not much will change in the direction of what you are experiencing. Pain, depression, anxiety, despair, anger, jealousy, are all *symptoms* of **fear**. Fear has a way of herding people.

We create our own problems when we refuse to take ownership for our mistakes. This affects the quality of our daily lives in ways we cannot see when we do not calmly take a step back and look. Fueled by emotion and insisting that we are right all the time is exactly the reason why we are facing such a difficult time in our lives. Some say *"it's just normal to feel bad."* Feelings that trigger emotions are like gauges and *check engine* lights on your dashboard! If you choose to ignore the signs that something *isn't right*, life will humble you. We cannot deny that it looks like we are in deep trouble, and it doesn't look like there is an end to the troubles we are about to face. At some point we must take *personal responsibility* for our <u>actions</u>, even if we chose to do nothing or just follow the herd *to fit in*.

If we now look at our behaviors on a global scale, we can see these same patterns at play. Technology is in evolutionary motion, and yet the highest budgets are spent on advancement of defense, military, and weapons of destruction. Wouldn't it make better sense if we spend more on the improvement of the human experience *instead*? How much defense would be needed if the world worked together to improve the quality of life for *everyone* on the planet? How much crime and violence would we see if more people were happy most of the time, and oppression *did not exist*? We create our own problems on a large scale by supporting those who put these current policies into action. It is as if we are trying to succeed at life using *self-sabotage* as a strategy. But keep reading...there is a logical reason why this happens.

More common than we would like

Humans have become creatures of habit. While change is a fact of life, a lot of us feel uncomfortable making major changes. However, subtle changes happen around us all the time. Sometimes we do not even pay attention until we notice something major happen.

Have you noticed road construction taking place, and all the sudden everything appears different, only once the road crews and barricades are all gone? Have you driven past a restaurant on the way to work every day, and then one day you just happened to look and it's gone? Have you ever driven home from somewhere completely sober and couldn't recall the details of the drive home?

The mind records everything, but it will send certain things to be filed for later use. Sometimes those nonimportant events will get purged, and sometimes the events are so traumatic that the mind will bury those memories in locked vaults for your own protection. It will usually take the help of a professional years to crack open that vault.

In order to experience something different, we will have to do something different. Remember, doing nothing is also a choice and sometimes it's the right one. In most cases doing nothing will usually return the same experience you are stuck in. It is very common to avoid change and just let the body run on auto-pilot. However, if a better quality of life is what we want, we must get out of the hole we are in right now, and that will require a well-planned and guided change.

Chapter 2:
Why Me?

There are times when it feels like I am being punished for something I didn't do. It is easy to give in to the feeling of pity and just quit caring. I'm not proud to admit it, but it happens. Those thoughts can make life seem hopeless if I entertain them for too long. A series of events may seem like the world is out to get me. If I channel my focus away from the negative thoughts, even for a moment, I will usually see there is always something I am missing. On the other hand, if I allow feelings of anger or pity to override my judgement, that's when everything goes sideways on me.

It's My Party

There is a song by Lesley Gore that became popular in 1964 about indulging in pity.[1] I don't recommend doing this, but as the song suggests: "*You would cry too if it happened to you.*" The truth is that you do have a choice.

Pity is a dangerous drug to be *high* on. It will take away any power you have to change your situation from a bad one to a good one, or even an *acceptable* one. Life will always throw a rock at you now and then. The trick is not to let one hit you, and there is a high probability a rock will hit you when you're not looking. So, staying alert and knowing how the mind works will prove to be a good strategy!

Those of us that can accept this fact of life, approach it with a sense of preparedness. We can always change our perspective if we want a better experience. Pity undermines any hope of finding a solution, as it burns away the positive perspective. All it offers you is negative energy... and that isn't where you will find solutions. Worry is also self-defeating

---

1   Erin Clements, "Woman who inspired 'It's My Party' reveals story behind the song's catchphrase," Today.com, last modified Feb. 20, 2015, accessed April 2, 2017, http://www.today.com/popculture/lesley-gores-its-my-party-story-behind-song-t4291

thought and behavior. Recall – *Thought and emotion are very powerful energy combined.* Well, action puts that energy into motion.

Depression and Anxiety

Depression and anxiety are what I call "in-house vampires" because the experience leaves me feeling drained of life, almost to the point of insanity. There are doctors that have offered me drugs in the past, but some of the side effects include suicidal *thoughts and tendencies*, which defeat the purpose of taking the medication for relief. There are tons of sources online that offer their opinions on depression, what causes it and how to overcome it. Doctors may also offer their own theories and opinions.

I am not a doctor, but I do know what depression feels like. And though my understanding of the brain is limited to what I can read about on websites and books, I rely mostly on my own experiences. Taking medications for every unpleasant event in my life isn't my first option, and has never been. I do know that sometimes medication is the fastest way towards relief. I also know that there are always better solutions to my problems than a quick fix. Personally, I must be careful relying on prescription medications. Casual use of these mind-altering drugs can lead even a non-addict down a very dark path. *For myself,* I always use that as the absolute last option. In many cases, I will endure the pain and try to ride it out as far as I can. This isn't for everyone, and I don't recommend you try this, but I know my own level of pain tolerance and what can happen if I let my usage get out of control. Also, my trust in the system of government-controlled medicine has diminished over the past several years. The year 2020 was when it became painfully obvious what was hiding in the shadows for an unsuspecting population.

Trust the Science

Many of us remember when the mainstream media, government, and a variety of alphabet agencies locked step and fed a bunch of lies to the world about a remedy to a manufactured virus unleashed on the world. We were told to *trust the science* and do not question authority, just take the shot. Many did, only to find out the harsh side effects included permanent and severe bodily damage and even premature death! Some doctors tried to warn us. Those who did were discredited, harassed, and in some cases dealt with in whatever means to become completely silenced. I guess if you look at the science of being silenced, that makes sense. Those who work in the shadows do not like the light of exposure on their work. There is logic to that. A lot of people compromised their integrity to avoid such unpleasantness, including scientists and *doctors*.

Addiction to Pharmaceuticals

The medical profession has become the medical industry. Not every doctor has your best interest at heart. Some do, but there are still those who take incentives from drug companies to put their patients on certain brands of medications. Don't be fooled... there is a huge market for "legal" drugs, and your doctor may become your dealer. Valium was introduced in 1963 and it reached $1 billion in sales. Xanax was introduced in 1981 and it became a hit to battle anxiety. Ritalin and Adderall have been prescribed to children as young as 4 years old.[2] No one is safe from drug abuse. Substance abuse among the elderly is also on the rise.[3]

A Personal Story

My father turned 87 years old this year (2021). Over the last few years, I've noticed his walking change from picking up his feet to shuffling them across the floor. His ability to comprehend is also diminishing. I justified it as just *old age*. It was to my dismay when I learned that his doctors were prescribing him **Temazepam** as a sleep aid. Also, every doctor he has seen over the *last twelve years*, has kept this old man on a drug that causes dizziness, confusion, and dementia! Temazepam is a drug that isn't recommended to take over a long period. The recommended time table is merely a few weeks. However, his doctors have kept prescribing

---

2   2 Chris Elkins, "Hooked on Pharmaceuticals: Prescription Drug Abuse in America," DrugWatch, last modified July 29, 2015, accessed April 5, 2017, https://www.drugwatch. com/2015/07/29/drug-abuse-in-america/.

3   Hazelden Betty Ford Foundation, "Substance Abuse Among the Elderly A Growing Problem," Hazelden Betty Ford Foundation, last modifiedMay11,2015,accessedApril 5, 2017, http://www. hazeldenbettyford.org/articles/substance-abuse-among-the-elderlya-growing-problem

this heavy narcotic *beyond* the point of substance abuse. *Who is at fault here?* Dad, for being addicted to the drug, or the doctors who are the gatekeepers and suppliers of it? What sense does it make to give an elderly person something with such harsh side effects? Wouldn't a *sleep study* be more beneficial?

Today, there is a drug for every single thought, emotion, and unpleasant event we experience in our lives. New drugs are being tested daily, to manage illnesses that do not have names yet. There are also new viruses still being cooked in laboratories in other parts of the world, and even here in America![4]

We shrug these events off as conspiracy theories, but are we this stupid, or is there something else in play that we *aren't aware of yet*? Maybe a second look might shed a little light on what is really going on? What purpose does gain-of-function research on bat coronaviruses serve?[5]

Decline of Human Condition Through Science and Medicine

The year 2020 is one that most of us will never forget. Not because our favorite team won a championship, but because this was the year when we were made aware of our ignorance to universal forces that shape our experience. Depression is a common problem for humans who don't quite understand their own power.

The suffering from depression and anxiety may only be from the thoughts and emotions we place on events that triggered it. In 2020 we created a situation for ourselves with little planning or thought, not even the use of basic science and biology... we let our fears lead us into an inferno! Now, scientists like, Geert Vanden Bossche[6], (*previously engaged with B. & M. Gates Foundation and GAVI*) are coming out and saying what we are doing could seriously wipe out humanity! What is going on?

---

4   Steven Salzberg, "Gain-Of-Function Experiments At Boston University Create A Deadly New Covid-19 Virus. Who Thought This Was A Good Idea?", Forbes, last modified Oct 24, 2022, accessed September 1, 2023, https://www.forbes.com/sites/stevensalzberg/2022/10/24/gain-of-function-experiments-at-boston-university-create-a-deadly-new-covid-19-virus-who-thought-this-was-a-good-idea/?sh=6533d4b55ca3

5   Fred Gutrel, "Dr. Fauci Backed Controversial Wuhan Lab with U.S. Dollars for Risky Coronavirus Research," Newsweek, last modified April 28, 2020, accessed March 18, 2021, https://www.newsweek.com/dr-fauci-backed-controversial-wuhan-lab-millions-us-dollars-risky-coronavirus-research-1500741?fbclid=IwAR0wf7e7ifeE7QPUqeUOs9SlzgY12QveTz4wSNH3exBSK1Gvq70jJqVWW_uU

6   https://be.linkedin.com/in/geertvandenbossche

We all witnessed together, the civil unrest, the violence, the lockdowns, everyone ordered to wear masks, disregard for facts or science, censorship and silencing of reputable doctors, social distancing (*what is social about distancing?*), a rigged Presidential election, exposure of criminal activity in every area of life; from The Church to The State, corruption without any sign of an end... and we are told this is the *new normal?* Could *that* be the cause of our depression?

Does it have to be a chemical imbalance in the brain that can only be corrected with drugs? Can we acknowledge actual causes of our depression and address it with an alternative remedy other than a chemical fix? Can we make a lifestyle change, or a change in mindset, or is taking a pill the best solution? These are questions only you as the individual can answer. Your doctor can help, but ultimately the one looking out for you, IS YOU. Your doctor is in business to make money. Sadly, your health is the way of profit here.

As for me, the feeling of being depressed is a good sign that I'm *down in the hole* again. I am very familiar with the feeling of being down. I am sure if my brain was under observation during those moments when I was at my lowest, some form of abnormalities would appear in the results. Somehow, I always seem to find a way out of my depression when I don't allow it to take over my mind. Focused and controlled breathing helps clear my thoughts. Meditation works wonders, and I use it more often than medication whenever possible. Being in full control of my own mind is important to me. Is it to you?

Early Humans and Depression

The ancients were not quick to run to the drug store for a fix. I find it unbelievable that cave people experienced less stress and problems than modern humans living in the developed world. There are still people today who live in conditions we consider unthinkable when compared to the lifestyle of Americans. We have Cadillac problems in contrast to most of the human population, and yet some of us just can't seem to find the will to live past our depression. One thing early humans did not practice was the glorification of our own weaknesses.

I know people who talk about their weaknesses like it is something worth celebrating. What is so great about painting yourself as a victim of life? Circumstances that can be avoided require open doors. Once you label yourself as a victim, options begin to vaporize as you slam the doors to opportunity shut. Early humans displayed strength because they had to. The harsh environment they existed in left them with little choice, unless they desired to become a meal for something or someone with more hunger and determination to survive.

It's hard for me to process how little we see, that the keys to better life experience is already in our own hand in the form of knowledge and experience. But sadly, we chose to complain about life instead of taking control of it. All we must do is seek a different mindset that will bring about a lifestyle change... one that we will *actually* enjoy.

Caveman Therapy

There are some essential things that will bring about a lifestyle change. These things have been used for many thousands of years to achieve great health and well-being. Some refer to this method of lifestyle change as the "caveman therapy."[7]

1. **Sunlight** – being out in the sun just feels better than being cooped up indoors for long periods of time. If you work indoors, take a break, and get out for a breath or two.
2. **Diet** – eating foods rich in Omega-3 fatty acids can lower the risk of heart disease, dementia, arthritis, and depression.
3. **Exercise** – getting regular daily exercise is a great way to stay in shape and shake off the cobwebs in the mind.
4. **Sleep** – getting enough sleep makes a huge difference. Without enough sleep, the body cannot function at its peak performance, and the mind can't stay focused.

---

7   Nicholas Kardaras Ph.D., "The Ancient Greek Cure for Depression and Anxiety," Psychology Today, last modified May 27, 2011, accessed April 15, 2017, https://www.psychologytoday.com/blog/how-plato-can-save-your-life/201105/the-ancient-greek-curedepression-and-anxiety

5. **Helping Others** – focusing on things that help others find their way out of a hole, flips the energy switch from negative to positive. Positive energy is what is needed to rise above depression.

6. **Social Activity** – social media does not count. Get out and meet people. Leave your phone in the car and enjoy time with a friend.

Ancient Greek Philosophy

"Men are disturbed not by events but by their opinions about them." This profound statement dates to ancient Greek philosophy. It is a line of wisdom from Stoic philosopher, Epictetus.[8] The Greeks believed that our emotions follow our beliefs. Emperor, Marcus Aurelius wrote: "The soul becomes dyed with the color of its thoughts." By changing your thoughts, you will change your experience.[9] The Greeks believed that philosophy, was itself, a form of therapy. Well, to me this makes sense because philosophy is a fancy word for *mentality*. Beliefs are powerful and are formed much like habits - by programming. The Greeks had many techniques for creating new habits. Their methods would target the ***subconscious mind***. Auto suggestion is one method to program the subconscious mind. American author, Napoleon Hill, mentions this technique in his best-selling self-help book, *Think and Grow Rich*.[10]

Exercising Choice

We all can rise above any situation that we face if we wanted to. Too many people make excuses why they "can't do" and fail to realize that by saying that, they have made their choice to quit before they even started. The *first* thought sets everything up for motion and manifestation.

Choice is a powerful force we have at our disposal, and it is ours to make. We always have more than one option, and as bad as the options may appear sometimes, there is always one that will work better for us at

8   Keith H. Seddon, "Epictetus (55–135 C.E.)," Internet Encyclopedia of Philosophy, 2014, accessed May 12, 2017, http://www.iep.utm.edu/epictetu/.

9   Jules Evans, "How ancient philosophy saved my life," Philosophy For Life, May 8, 2012, accessed May 3, 2017, http://www.philosophyforlife.org/times-piece-on-ancientphiloso-phy-cbt-and-the-politics-of-well-being/.

10   Napoleon Hill, Think and Grow Rich, (Meriden, CT: The Ralston Society 1938), OpportunityInformer. co

that time. Making a choice that will improve our life takes practice and the willingness to change.

For example, if one seeks a less stressful environment to live in, a lifestyle change can yield better living conditions. This option may require relocation or a change in job, or maybe even a change in acquaintances and/ or friends. It will most likely require an exit strategy. This requires effort and some discomfort, and is usually why many of us lack the *willingness* to change. However, it is the willingness to make the change that will make the difference. One very important thing to remember about change is that **change is all there is**. It is in the *resistance* of it where pain is experienced.

Life will always throw you a curve at some point. Waking up in a hole is a common point of view for us all (*some more than others*). Those who seem to always have the luck to land safely, maybe do...or maybe they have mastered the art of falling. *Perspective* is the key to changing one's own experience, according to the Greeks. Their wisdom has been used for centuries since it was first cited. I believe, like the ancients, that it is choice of perspective that makes a very dark place seem like the way to an exit.

Everyone has an opinion, and yours always comes from your perspective. A few things we all need to remember here are: First, we all have different perspectives. Next, the view from a mountain top is much different than the one in the valley. And most importantly, you must *climb* for that mountain top view! The choice to remain ignorant has never resulted well for anybody since the beginning of time. I'm sure back then there were extreme challenges too, but technology today has opened more doorways to hell than we can count! Instead of using technology to better the experience of all humans, we are choosing to kill ourselves off with it.

Chapter 3:
It's Not My Fault and Other Excuses

Do you ever feel like you are being attacked when others bring an error in judgement to your attention? I must admit, I do not like being accused of any wrong doings, even when I am wrong. Who does? Once the dust and smoke settles, the fingers come out, and the pointing begins. Everyone is looking for the at-fault party, but no one is looking inward. We all fall short somewhere and like to blame someone or something else. We say things like: "*It's not my fault*," then make some random excuse. Later, we are visited again with another similar crisis to deal with. We cannot control the forces of nature, but if we do our part to take precautions, we will not have as much tragedy as we see today. Carelessness is on us to control. Let us begin to examine this deeper by looking at something we do every day without much self-reflection... driving

Accident or Incident?

I experienced too many auto-related "*accidents*" in my early career as a young and irresponsible driver. When the police arrive, the pointing begins with the words "*It's not my fault.*" The wreckage left behind after a car-crash is not something people are quick to claim responsibility for. Also, it's not recommended that you speak too much before your *insurance company* has a chance to investigate first.

The feeling after experiencing this traumatic event is something hard to describe with words. Emotions are mixed with feelings of anger and guilt, sorrow, and despair. If there are injuries, these feelings are amplified. We all want to throw the blame on the other driver, but for a collision to take place, both drivers had to be negligent to some degree. That's right...both drivers have a part in a collision. Of course, sometimes there is nothing that can be done to avoid a crash, other than to brace for it. Although most of the time this is *not* the case.

Even though the "at-fault" party made the move that caused the crash, the one who was hit also had options that could have avoided the wreck. As a result of being the "at-fault" driver, my driving experience today has improved so much, that I have avoided many potential crashes. Some instances were too close for my level of comfort, and could have ended very badly. I am grateful to be alert enough to act the way I did to avoid the worst case in these situations.

In our society, drinking alcohol, taking drugs, and driving under the influence was a problem for decades, and still is today. But now we have a bigger problem with driving under the influence of technology. Today, people are on their phones all the time. Talking on the phone is distracting while one is driving. Bluetooth technology has made phone conversations a little safer behind the wheel, so the irresponsible driver had to find a better way to put everyone's life at risk again.

Now, instead of using the Bluetooth device people are texting while they are driving. Some people take pictures or video of themselves while they are driving. Even though this activity is extremely hazardous and foolish, the people who do it have an excuse to justify their ridiculous behavior. Some claim to be "really good at it." Others say that they can multi-task better than others. A few people will admit that it is risky behavior, but they will do it anyway.

The statistics clearly show how dangerous this activity is, and yet some states allow it to go on without penalty under their traffic laws. These careless acts usually result in severe injury, dismemberment, or death to those who fall victim to these negligent drivers. And careless drivers are on every street, back road, highway, and parking lot across every city in the country.

More than 2.5 million Americans were injured from motor vehicle collisions in 2012, according to federal government report.[11] 1.6 million

---

11   Sam P.K. Collins, "Americans to the Emergency Room Every Year," Think Progress, October 10, 2014, accessed August 10, 2016, https://thinkprogress.org/car-accidentssend- 2-5-million-americans-to-the-emergency-room-every-year-b81b191a09b8/.

incidents are caused by cell phone use every year.[12] And that number is growing annually. This means more than half of the road collisions in the US involve cell phones. Texting and driving are 6 times more likely to get you in an "accident" than drunk driving.[13]

If this is scary, then stop doing it, and stop it when you see it. We are all guilty at some point. A careless driver is not focused on the task of driving his/her vehicle safely. Careless drivers do not have accidents... they *cause* incidents, and they do it *willfully*.

Justifying Poor Judgement

Driving a big truck for a living is a dangerous job. I have spent a good amount of my life on the roads and highways. Trailers are everywhere you look on the roads we drive on. Since we share the roads, it's important to know a few things about each other. Having this knowledge will help if we don't want to become a casualty, or to make someone else become one.

Cars can stop quickly if they need to. Large vehicles cannot. The weight of a vehicle determines its safe braking distance. When a small car zips into that safe brake zone, the careless driver of that car is making a willful decision, that can claim lives, cause bodily injury, and property damage. We see this too often, and yet people still think this behavior is acceptable. People seem to not have the capacity to learn from the poor judgement of others. Even when that poor judgement results in carnage.

We often hear about wrong way drivers,[14] and we view video footage of horrific head-on collisions involving a drunk or careless driver. Even though we can see the results of the aftermath, still there are those who are in too much of a hurry to follow simple safety measures. These people will risk the lives of others, along with their own, as they cross into oncoming lanes. I've seen people do this around blind curves and other no-pass zones, only to shorten their trip time by a few minutes.

12   Stephanie Haines, "Report: Cell phone distraction causes one in four US car crashes," The Christian Science Monitor, January 12, 2010, accessed August 10 2016, https://www.cs-monitor.com/USA/2010/0112/Report-Cell-phone-distraction-causesone-in-four-US-car-crashes.

13   Luke Ameen, "The 25ScariestTextingandDrivingAccidentStatistics," ICEBIKE, accessed August 5, 2016, http://www.icebike.org/texting-and-driving/.

14   Mark Doctor, "Wrong Way Driving: New Focus on a Persistent Problem," TRB Webinar, Federal Highway Administration Resource Center, April 20, 2016, accessed January 3, 2017, http://onlinepubs.trb.org/Onlinepubs/webinars/160420.pdf

Wrong-way driving is a huge problem across the entire country. Arizona alone recorded more than 1600 incidents in 2016.[15] Every state is doing what they can to address this deadly problem. Why is it so hard to get people to realize wrong-way driving is deadly? If you have the capacity to drive, shouldn't that include the ability to make rational decisions? Is it rational to point your vehicle *against* the flow of traffic?

We become frustrated while we sit in gridlocked traffic caused by a careless driver, but a few days later *we* become the careless one. This inability to learn from what we experience is perplexing, but there is a simple reason we do it. We justify our actions and just move on, regardless of how bad our actions may be, or how many lives it could affect. A simple justification will turn poor judgement into acceptable behavior, and it will be recorded as such in the mind. It works just like that. We will be doomed to repeat that behavior until we change our thoughts about it, and view it as *unacceptable*.

Understanding the Ego
Another thing we should be aware of is ego. Our *ego* is strong enough to justify anything and most of us aren't aware of its presence. Ego is created within the mind's software and works in the dark for a reason. But if we are aware of its presence and understand its value, we could gain from its use. I wrote another book that explains the ego in full detail. It also identifies the spirit, or *soul* and how to tell the difference between the two (*spirit versus ego*). That book is called ***Highest Self: A Book of Powerful Secrets to Leash the Ego***. If you want to know more about the ego and how it plays each and every one of us, I recommend that you read that one too! A lot of work went into that book too. Information about the ego is scattered an obscure. However, I managed to find enough to piece together a clear image of what ego is and how it can be useful.

---

15   KTAR, "More than 1,600 wrong-way driving incidents reported in Arizona," KTAR News, lastmodifiedDecember14,2016, accessed January3,2017, https://ktar.com/story/1390272/ arizona-dps-over-1600-wrong-way-driving-incidentsreported-to-dps-this-year/

Preventing the Preventable

Unaware of ego, people make all kinds of excuses when it comes to their bad driving habits. Some people will blame their behavior on an argument with their partner. Running late for work, picking up the kids, or meeting someone is never a good reason to risk a collision. Some people blame their carelessness on a bad day at work, having to go to the bathroom, having to let their dogs in from the rain, or they just deny being careless. They will use whatever excuse necessary to get them out of a traffic fine. People who are too busy to care about their own safety aren't going to care about yours. If one is sincere about avoiding the pitfalls of life, prevention then becomes possible.

It's no wonder so many people lose their lives in exchange for convenient transportation. Driving is something most of us have to do in order to earn a living. Some people drive for a living. The more you are on the roads, the more you are at risk. It shouldn't have to be this way, and it wouldn't be this way if more people accepted responsibility for their actions. If you think you couldn't make a difference, think again. Every person has the power to change the world by first changing themselves.

Smokey Says It Is Your Fault

Wild fires occur almost every year in dry areas of the country. Some of it is caused by lightning, but then there are those that are caused by the actions of irresponsible people. I have witnessed on many occasions, where the driver in front of me will flick a lit cigarette out of a moving car window. During a dry spell, that lit cigarette could be the cause of a major fire.

Irresponsibility is the major cause of many of the problems we face today. People just don't want to claim what is theirs, unless there is a victory attached at the end. For this reason, we will never be able to overcome the problems we face. If we are to change our world for the better, we must start with ourselves first. We must take an honest look at our part in every bad situation, and figure out why we think it is okay.

Is burning down thousands of acres of land that is not yours, okay? Is placing the lives of hundreds of emergency workers at risk, okay? Is causing innocent people to risk losing their homes and everything they work to have, okay? If you see these things not being okay, then think about this the next time you throw a lit cigarette out of your window. Think about this when you are having fun playing with fireworks in dry conditions. Your intent may not be to cause harm, but your actions will.

A Burning City

There is a small mining town in Pennsylvania that is said to be burning from underground for many decades. Centralia is known throughout the state as the burning city.[16] No one knows for sure how the fire started, but some believe it started as careless trash burning in a landfill next to an open pit mine, which ignited a coal vein. As the fire spread further throughout the town underground, hot poisonous gases came through the basements of homes and businesses. The government eventually stepped in and bought up the property and relocated the residents.[17]

16   Courtney Barrow, "Centralia, Pennsylvania: How an underground mine fire turned a thriving community into an eerie ghost town," AccuWeather, March 31, 2017, accessed June 20, 2017, https://www.accuweather.com/en/weather-news/ghost-town- exploredcentralias-mine-fire-smolders-300-feet-below-an-eerie-abandoned-land- scape/70001172.
17   Roadside America Team, "Centralia Mine Fire," RoadsideAmerica.com, accessedJune20, 2017, http://www.roadsideamerica.com/story/2196.

Centralia, Pennsylvania 2015

Although there are still a few people who chose to stay in this city in ruin, the conditions in Centralia continue to decline. No one knows how much longer the fire will continue to burn. Some estimate another 250 years before the fire runs out of fuel. Whenever that time comes, the damage has already been done. The environment will never be the same as a result of someone's negligence. Passing the blame will not bring life back to Centralia, nor will it teach people the valuable and expensive lesson there is to learn there. As we continue to dodge responsibility for our actions, more damage will be the result. One day we could wake up to our very own Centralia... unless we change our thoughts and behaviors now.

A Hard Look

There are those that look to profit from every resource on the planet. Their agenda doesn't involve saving lives. Although the narrative may include something about saving your grandma or the future of your children, *for the greater good*...the money trail will have more to tell than the talking heads you see on TV. Critical thinkers are labeled as *conspiracy theorists* that are a danger to national security because nothing can get past a critical thinking mind without questions.

It's hard to know for sure just how much damage we are doing to our world by our carelessness. One thing is for sure…it isn't stopping. We continue to press forward with policies that are proven to fail. During moments when we can see the result of those failed policies, we choose to look away. This kind of lackadaisical behavior is what ends civilizations. Do we think we are different, better, or smarter? YES? Those who perished before us thought so too. Humans cannot trick science. Science is the law of nature, and will not bend or be broken. Believe in them or not, they will continue to be, long after we are gone.

Global Warming

Global warming is a hot topic in the news all over the world. Some countries take it more seriously than others. The issue of global warming can easily be measured if we apply simple math and science to find an answer. Unfortunately, we have chosen to apply politics instead. Social media has played a big part recently in shaping public opinion. However, science and math will yield a better and more accurate answer than bloggers and media "experts" with specific agendas, political memes, and other propaganda shared with friends on social media. Uneducated and politically charged people spread misinformation around as facts. These people think they are doing what is right, but they are feeding into the plans of those who carelessly continue to poison our world. The idea of lessening the carbon footprint was lost when the decision was made to mandate electric vehicles[18] and to incinerate dangerous chemicals into the atmosphere.[19] Both of these known and documented events prove

18 Dan Gearino, "California Just Banned Gas-Powered Cars. Here's Everything You Need to Know," Inside Climate News, last modified September 1, 2022, accessed September 1, 2023, https://insideclimatenews.org/news/01092022/california-just-banned-gas-powered-cars-heres-everything-you-need-to-know/

19 Aria Bendix, "High levels of a hazardous chemical polluted the air weeks after the Ohio train derailment, an analysis shows," NBC Health News, last modified July 12, 2023, accessed September 1, 2023, https://www.nbcnews.com/health/health-news/ohio-train-derailment-hazardous-chemical-polluted-air-rcna93640

that those who use climate change to gain public approval care nothing about the atmosphere, safe water, the soil, or anything else that protects the environment or makes living conditions possible.

The arguments from both sides of the global warming debate are compelling. Answers can easily be obtained, but only if we look at the hard facts. Choosing to ignore the facts does not change the truth, and choosing to refer to politics as "science" will not change the difference between the two either. If we don't learn *how* to think and only rely on what we are told to think, we will find ourselves in a lot of trouble! We are only seeing a glimpse of what is coming. *Totalitarianism* is real and the experience is very harsh. Every regime that has gained full control of its people started out the same way. *For the greater good...*

The Phenomenon of Life

If we only pick the facts we like and discount those we do not, we are in for a rude awakening. Nature does not play games with humans. In fact, the forces of nature are far more powerful than a stubborn human. Look at the power of wind and what it can do. Wind can allow an airplane to fly for thousands of miles. Wind can also pick up a tanker truck and throw it across hundreds of feet of roadway. Wind can move ships across oceans. Wind can also turn a house into a pile of splinters the size of toothpicks. Water is the essence of life, and yet it has the power to take life. Likewise, without fire, humankind wouldn't be able to exist, and yet fire can also be a destroyer of life.

We may never find all the answers to the mysteries of life. However, we should consider the risk involved before we decide to act and make it a part of our life experience. The phenomenon of life will always be a mystery, but we can choose to learn from our pitfalls. Choosing to live with risk in our lives is all part of the human experience. We shouldn't be afraid to live life to its fullest. However, taking calculated risks is a smarter way to do this. But, managing risks requires a working and open mind... also the effort required to become self-informed. Truth is not going to be found all on the surface. Most of it you will need to dig for, then piece together yourself, sort of like a puzzle. Your mind must be open and in tune with what makes sense. Also, intuition is always accurate if one uses it often enough. My gut feelings have never failed me... ever.

Feeling Safe Versus Being Safe

The number of people who lose their lives to auto incidents overshadow those who die from firearms. Unfortunately, there seems to be a large gap between those who politicize the issue of gun control and those who are intending to save human lives. As ignorance and misinformation flood the mainstream news and social media, the debate over feeling safe versus being safe continue to further blind the people in favor of stricter gun control measures.

If we look at the number of auto incidents involving an impaired driver, we can see that the common factor in all those situations was the *operator* and not the vehicle. So, why is it so hard to accept that it's the *shooter* that is responsible for his actions and not the weapon of choice?

We see politicians use victims to push an agenda to ban certain firearms. The "news" or mainstream media is all over it, unless the shooter was taken out by an armed citizen. There is so much programming going on around us, that it even affects the most intelligent people. Those that are not aware of the mind tricks are pulled into the vortex of lies and propaganda through psychological warfare. *Ideological subversion*[20] tactics are evident in what we are seeing in both mainstream and social media in 2021.

We live in a primal society. We lack the ability to be civil to one another. We live in a society driven by fear, and that has its side effects. Some of the people resort to crime as their way of life, and as we live among these criminals, we become their targets. But the criminal activity does not stop at the lower end of the economic ladder either.

The evil in our world can be found at the very top to the very bottom, and everywhere in between. This is our world now, and we must

---

20 "FULL INTERVIEW with Yuri Bezmenov: The Four Stages of Ideological Subversion (1984)," YouTube video, 1:21:28, Posted by "Nicholas Marshall," August22, 2020, https:// www.youtube.com/ watch?v=yErKTVdETpw.

find a way to live in it safely. Handing over what is left of our freedoms and rendering ourselves completely defenseless isn't a *rational* choice. Handing over our rights to a criminal element is even a worse idea.

Merely a Tool

Firearms have a place under these circumstances. I understand why an armed society is a good idea. There is so much corruption everywhere. Without a means to protect my family, friends, and neighbors (who are not armed) *makes us all potential victims*. We are literally waiting our turn to become the next group of statistics, unless we have the tools to stop that from happening. Firearms are merely tools. If we look back at the tools, we used a century ago, most of them are obsolete simply because society out grew the need for them, or we built better ones. Well, the weapons of the modern age are far more destructive than the firearms that are in debate. Wouldn't it make more sense to look for other ways to render the firearm obsolete? I mean There are better uses for flying projectiles than killing each other... isn't there? Shooting at clays never killed anyone, that exercised proper safety protocol.

It seems like the whole world would rather grasp at straws instead of solving the real problems. But that isn't what's happening here. Auto suggestion is a technique used to penetrate ideas into beliefs through the *subconscious mind*. I will explain this further in the last section of this book.

For now, it's important to know that evil in our world *does* exist. The plan makers are so clever and unscrupulous, that signs of their intentions are right out in the open and their plans were kept well-hidden until now. These so-called "world leaders" have given themselves the authority to violate our basic human rights and are steering our societies towards absolute and total human enslavement! But this is not the first time. Psychological warfare is *hacking* into the minds of the masses to manipulate control of the collective conscious. The "would-be" victims are faithfully carrying the plan into play without a *single* doubt. To an objective observer, it looks like a sleepwalker walking its way right off a cliff!

Responsibility Under Fire

In a society where people are kind to one another, respect each other, and look out for the common good of everyone, there would not be a need for firearms. Look around... do you see that happening anywhere? We have a long way to go, but it is possible to achieve such advancement in consciousness.

First, we must learn to take responsibility for our own actions. We need to see that making excuses only prolongs the pain, and places us further from where we want to be. We must find another way out of our hole. Making changes that we know are useless, will not solve our problems. We must move past our beliefs and set aside our emotions to find lasting solutions. We must come together as a society united. A nation of free thinkers instead of divided people with *poisoned* minds. The sickness resides on both sides of the great divide.

The gun debate has become stale. A good start to put an end to that debate would be to create a society that renders the gun obsolete. Get together with your family, friends and neighbors and find some common ground. Then, reach out as a group to other groups to share ideas and unite as active citizens with a *common* goal... **peace and prosperity for all**.

The Cost of Freedom is Paid in Blood

I believe this is how America started. The idea that people that are united, indivisible with liberty and justice for all came with a price. The gun was simply a tool that helped make this idea stick, and it continues to be the tool that keeps this idea the law of the land. With the way the world is going now, it seems as if this tool is still necessary in the hands of a population that is against relentless oppression by an overreaching "*government*." There is no doubt that's what is going on right now. Those *elected* are taking their orders from *unelected* special interest groups. The people of this nation are no longer in control of their own government that is selling them into slavery.

That is why the framers of the ***Declaration of Independence*** made sure to include this detail as a *right* that *shall not be infringed* by government. Infringement by government is evident in every policy made by the unlawful corporation that has masked itself as the *authority*. Under the *highest* jurisdiction on US soil, members of an organization working to dismantle the human rights of its own people would be seen as *criminals*. Then, arrested and charged with the crime of treason, and then punished severely for their *abuse* of power. Tools will be needed to do this and we have a lot of work ahead of us, if we want our future generations to enjoy the freedoms we never had. A day may come where this tool will be rendered obsolete, but that day isn't today. Freedom, liberty, peace, prosperity, and mutual respect. These things will render the firearm obsolete. Isn't that what we should all *shoot* for?

Claiming the Blame

Pointing blame and making excuses to justify poor judgement only results in more poor judgement. Catastrophic losses are usually related to poor judgment. To really get better end results, we must stop lying to ourselves and accept our pitfalls as what they are. To move past the hole requires claiming the responsibility for our own judgements, beliefs, and actions. Failure to do so will only create more of the same kind of problems.

Allowing our ego to run like a tornado and leaving the destruction for others to deal with, isn't going to get us out of a hole. That is foolish mentality, and thinking like a fool will only make the hole deeper. Too many people think it's easier to run from responsibility and let someone else deal with their mess. Most people do this unconsciously, reacting to their hidden fears and emotional programming. Unbeknownst to them, they appear as the fool to those who have the vantage point of logic. Fortunately, foolishness has a remedy. But it is up to the individual to recognize and correct the behavior.

By using our intellect instead of reacting to our emotions, we can own our mistakes and this will turn the bad in our lives into something good. When we accept our part of the failure, we put ideas into motion that will direct us away from future failure. This process breaks the chain of the "*business as usual*" mentality, and how the *subconscious mind* is reprogrammed. As the old programs are erased, new programs are written over them. Every time we do this, we are closer to our desired position in life.

It's in the subconscious part of the mind where all of our thinking and behavior patterns are stored. If you often wonder: *why did I just do that?* Those behaviors are programmed, so are thought patterns. So, if you think you have no control of your thoughts, think again. It's important to know the subconscious mind is a powerful tool, and one that we mustn't misuse.

The purpose of this book is to explain the subconscious side of the mind, and how easily it can be hacked. It's quite scary to think that your mind can be hacked easily like your phone or computer. Technology seems to be squeezing out the human element. Social engineers have never had it so easy! What took centuries to keep masked while pushing forward now can be done in a matter of months! 2020 was proof of that. The time to wake up is long past. We are about to go into crisis again if we are not able to gain control of our own subconscious. Because, that is where the war is taking place.

Chapter 4:
Getting Out by Digging In

When you find yourself in a hole, the first thought that comes to mind isn't "*how did I get here?*" but rather, how am I going to get out? Getting out of the hole will require a different way of thinking than the one used to fall in. Not falling into the same hole over and over, requires one to acknowledge the steps leading up to the fall. This way of critical thinking is not a very popular choice because it requires one to own their errors and poor choices.

I can say without hesitation, that I don't like the feeling of knowing that I was the cause of grief for someone else. I will also admit that I don't like to admit guilt, especially when I was the cause of my own grief. This is common among all humans. Nobody likes to admit they're wrong. Looking inward is rare, but it's the fastest way out of a hole, because inward is where our power can be found and also where the control mechanisms are.

The Looking Glass
Looking inward for answers, opens the doorway to one of the most powerful tools in the human arsenal... insight. This is the all-knowing, all-seeing eye, that we all have but rarely use. Insight is the key to God-like wisdom and power. Humans come equip with this amazing tool, but sadly, most don't even take it out of the package.

Insight has many benefits. Several years ago, I read about meditation and the divine wisdom one can find from within. I then tried it and experienced a series of profound understandings. Today, I can quiet my mind and reach that place of wisdom through meditation. I had to first learn that to get to the root of any problem I had to dig deeper than the surface, because solutions are always at the root level. Only problems... and more problems are found on the surface. Most of the time, all I need to do is quiet my mind and dig in. It's in this crucial process where solutions are found. Long-lasting solutions don't come from quick fixes. This process takes time to learn, and even longer to master. With awareness, practice, and determination, we can learn to use the gift of insight to achieve great things. It has been said that *those who don't go within, go without.*

Taking the First Steps

It was Albert Einstein that said: "We cannot solve our problems with the same thinking we used when we created them."[21] Changing your thinking patterns isn't going to be easy. Thinking and behavior patterns have been programmed into our subconscious mind since before we were aware of it, and that goes back to our early childhood. We still run on some of those programs to this day.

To change the way we think and behave, we need to change those programs to something more fitting to the way we want to live. We must be open to new ideas and become willing to try them. Open mindedness and willingness are two essential elements in this formula. Without either of these two, we are going to battle ourselves into failure. There are many tools at our reach, once we open ourselves to the possibilities outside of our own thinking. If what we are thinking and doing have left us feeling unsatisfied, then changing our thoughts and actions only makes sense. That first step is the toughest to take, but once that first step is taken, our life will begin to change instantly, even if we can't see it yet.

Change Is All There Is

Everything in life is in a constant state of change. Nothing stays the same. We are either moving forward or moving backward. That's why it sometimes feels like we are taking a step forward and two steps back. Those last two steps are only setbacks in life, but if we continue with that backward trend, we will find ourself in a hole.

---

21   DavidMielach,"5 Business Tips from Albert Einstein, "Business News Daily, last modified April 18, 2012, accessed March 11, 2018, https://www.businessnewsdaily.com/2381-al- bert-einstein-business-tips.html.

Change is painful for many people to accept, but the pain is only in the resistance, and not the change. This is a law of nature that is working in the background and applies to the entire universe. It happens every second of every single day. Accepting change is another *crucial* step towards **life mastery**.

Once you understand this powerful law of nature, a lot of things begin to happen. You will find that you have incredible abilities through your thoughts, words, and actions to make the desired changes in your life. Also, sometimes the things we see as problematic are needed changes that realign our path to our desires. By our stubborn refusal to accept these changes, we are actually *undermining* our own path to happiness.

Hidden Truths

Once we get past the discomfort of our fears, we will be able to see with our sixth sense. This is where we begin to see a truth so well hidden that many will never get a glimpse. Most people never look past the surface level for anything. If you try to have a meaningful conversation with them, they will back off, shut down, or become offended. At the very least you will hear them say something like: "That's way too deep for me." Or "I just keep it simple." I hear things like that more now than ever before.

My Personal Experience

I have a friend that I have known for many years. He and I share a very common bond. A few years ago, he ended a very self-destructive path by going to jail. After several months of incarceration, he decided to continue exercising his old thinking and behavior patterns that landed him in jail. This time he ended up in a hospital bed. After an unintentional overdose, he finally decided to change his behaviors for a while.

I offered once again to help him, to which he replied: "*I got this.*" He made it clear to me that my views and his are different. I agreed. He said that people can have different opinions and still get along. Once again, I agreed.

People are different. Some choose to stay misinformed, and others choose to seek the truth. Those who seek truth will always see beyond the false barriers that stand in front of those still in the dark. Being in the dark is a choice. The darkness hides all of life's treasures. Some people say that ignorance is bliss. I can't seem to put the two together. Ignorance is a liability. That's all it is. Ignorance never excused anyone from the law, and it will never excuse one from personal responsibility. Ignorance is only a choice.

To better the quality of your life, you must look deeper at yourself. You have to be willing to take the steps necessary to succeed. This includes seeking out the light of truth, even if it makes you feel uncomfortable at first. The feeling of discomfort is your eyes adjusting to the light. Being in the dark for so long, sometimes we forget that the light exists. But, seeking the light is also a choice, and so is being the light.

The world is a dark place, because, to appreciate our true form requires contrast. I've said this in other books, ***we are light energy in the form of solid matter***. That is the physical human form. That much is science, as for the rest...hidden truths are everywhere you look. You just need to calibrate your compass and safeguard your *subconscious*. Life is an adventure in all directions!

Chapter 5:
A Much Larger Problem

Everything is much different than it seems to appear. The eyes can deceive what we think is real. What appears to be real is only our perceived reality. With enough thought and belief, we make it real and manifest it into physical reality. We rely way too much on our five senses that we hardly ever use our *sixth sense*. It is only through the sixth sense that we can actually see what is really going on behind the curtain.

Stuck in Our Own Beliefs

This is a huge problem, but also a very common one. We are taught to think and believe certain things that categorize us as "good" Christian, Muslim, or Jewish people. In addition to that, we are also told that we need to pick a political side - right wing or left wing - and support those points of view. Then, if we are dark-skinned or light-skinned, we have the tendency to only mingle with our own kind.

It is through this process of division that we lose our sense of oneness. The fact that we are all spirit beings and come from the same source is ignored by the rule of man. We all have the capacity to love and be loved, yet somehow, we fall into this cycle of lies that we're all different. As we continue to believe it, our societies mold us into thinking and reacting through fear. Most of us are still unconscious to this as we are unaware of the *ego* that is used to manipulate our thinking process. Once you actually wake up, you realize that your whole life has been one huge lie. Then the reprogramming towards the truth can begin. But until then, the conditioning process continues to keep the masses in a dark hole.

Belief is a powerful tool if it's used correctly. It can create anything we want to make real. However, our programmed beliefs can be our biggest liability. Believing in the lies we are told, and those we tell ourselves is a set up for a lifetime of darkness. We may think everything is fine, but there is nothing good to gain from living a life of lies.

Many people are stuck in their beliefs and can't get past them. Accepting that we are living a life of lies scares people. Our whole existence is based on a lie? That would mean we have to start over and reevaluate everything. *Yes.* That would take a lot of time and work. *Yes, it would.* Why would we want to do that? *Because the effort would be worth making.* That fear of change is something that has become normal human behavior. But, avoiding change is not *natural* to the order of universal law.

Normal Versus Natural

What we classify as being normal isn't always natural. Our nature as a human being is to grow and evolve. Anything in the way of that evolution is not natural. Most of us resist change. That is also not natural. Change is the only constant in our lives. Change is all there is, yet so many of us are uncomfortable with it. Why is that? We have forgotten who and what we are, and this is a much larger problem. We have accepted what is considered normal as what is natural. Our ideas of the way life should be, is defying nature...that's a huge problem.

The holes we place ourselves in are a direct result of our ignorance of these laws of nature. Ignorance has never excused anyone from man-made laws. Nature's rule of law is not negotiable. It is divine and governs the entire universe. Like them or not, it is what it is.

In order to have control over our own lives, we must know who and what we are. We must know what we want, and who we want to be. Being normal doesn't bring us closer to that idea. In fact, it takes us further away from ever asking those questions. Being normal places us in a herd of mindless human livestock, where evolution and growth cease to exist. Now we are calling mindlessness the "new normal" ...? Who are we kidding here?

Control of Your Mind

Mind control has been going on since the beginning of time. The ruling class have been keeping the masses of people under control in order to secure their own positions of wealth and power. They have procured this through research, development of ideas, and years of continued testing. We have been the test subjects of mind control programs for so long, and yet most of us don't even know it. Those that deny it are victims of their own ego. Make no mistake, we are all involved in a silent attack of our minds to steer our collective consciousness.

Psychological warfare is powerful science. ***Ideological Subversion*** is *real* and very dangerous if we remain ignorant to its existence in our systems of media, government, and military. This process has been kept secret, but signs of it are quite obvious. There are people that sense something sinister is going on. Most "normal" people are blind to it, and may even think of those that aren't normal as conspiracy nuts for thinking such thoughts. We will take a deeper look into mind control tactics used by governments to manipulate their people in *chapter 11*. But for now, it's important to know that your subconscious mind is constantly under attack.

If you've ever had a bad Trojan or Worm virus on your computer, then you will become horrified at how easy it is to gain entry to your mind through the use of new and old technology. Some techniques are so effective, they have been in use for centuries, and from empire to empire. Fear is a powerful human emotion that even the ancients were made aware of. Fear has become instinctual as a result of our fascination with it. What we haven't been able to process as a collective consciousness, is that fear is the driving force to our own demise, and also the absence of love and faith. Instead of embracing love and faith, we glorify fear instead and weave it into the fabric of our culture like a cancer. What purpose does a *culture of fear* serve?

Culture of Fear

Take a look around and you will see that everything is motivated by fear. The mainstream media use fear campaigns to push political agendas.

They also use fear tactics to push products and services in the form of advertising. Religions have used fear mongering for centuries in the form of torture, imprisonment, and even death.[22]

We are told that if we refuse to believe and obey their rules our souls will burn in a place called hell. Some people don't believe in such nonsense, but others are gripped with fear, so much so, that they are stuck in their way of thinking.

Humans even glorify fear. Here in the US, we have a special holiday in October where it is customary to wear costumes. People dress up as ghouls, skeletons and zombies and take to the streets. Haunted houses are set up to scare the crap out of paying visitors. But this is just one example. A grimmer look at our fascination with fear is noticeable just by going shopping. Everyone, it seems like, is hiding behind a mask.

Some have embraced this *unnatural* behavior as necessary to keep from spreading germs. Without understanding the science, I guess fear could paralyze one's thinking subliminally. But that is why we need to be aware of subversion techniques. Without question, evil does exist outside of movies. Our fears should be focused hard on that element rather the ones put right in front of us to look at. Movies and television shows are called projects and programs *literally*.

Horror movies have become so popular that there are thousands to choose from. There are killer films about real life serial killers, or fictional characters like movie monsters from blood-sucking vampires to werewolves, and even a beast made from spare body parts. There are so many ways we glorify fear, and yet we never even see how this has had an effect on us.

Blood and gore pique our interest to the point of huge traffic jams around minor fender-benders. A traffic incident scene where there are signs of a fatality can stop traffic for hours. Everyone wants to see the sight of blood, and if there is an opportunity to take a picture or shoot a video to show our friends... *hey, why not?*

---

22   "Secret Files of the Inquisition–part(s)1-4," YouTubevideo,201:28(combined), post- ed by "Kings of Docs," Jan 30, 2015, https://www.youtube.com/watch?v=r_CbjGM3_Fo&t=2s.

One Small Step to Freedom

When looking at the bigger picture, we can see that there is a much larger problem at work here. What we initially thought was the problem has roots deeper than just the surface level. Our thoughts and behaviors have been programmed long before we were old enough to question any of it. As children, we don't have very much say in what we are told to do or even believe. But as adults the rules change and so do the availability of choices. If we continue to run on the same programs that we have had since childhood, there are going to be pitfalls along the way. Our parents didn't program us to fail in life. They did the best they could with what they had. As adults, we now have a choice to question everything and see if it still fits. If you think that everything is fine the way it is, just consider that without further knowledge there is no more growth. Think of things that are still out there for you to discover...? I am only assuming that by reading this deep into this book, there had to have been a life event that landed you in a hole. Finding yourself in a hole isn't an uncommon event. It gets the best of us at some point. I can say with confidence that to find freedom in this lifetime, one must break free of all beliefs and leave no walls around the mind. Only a mind wide open to all possibilities will grant access to unlimited freedom. Exploration of the universe is possible, but only with a mind without boundaries. This doesn't mean without responsibility. Personal responsibility is always in the equation. And, this all starts with one small step, but the freedom that comes with that first step is *huge*.

SECTION 2

Freedom

Chapter 6:
Courage

Most people think that to do something courageous requires an act of incredible bravery. Well, that's partially true. When I say partially, I mean that it does require one to act in spite of their own fear. You don't necessarily have to run into a flaming building to save a baby to be courageous. It can be something as simple as overcoming the fear of change.

It takes courage to accept change. Courage decimates fear and opens the doorway to freedom. Courage is the key to life itself. Without this crucial element, we are nothing more than victims. Anything, anyone, and every situation we face will require courage to some degree.

There are times that we stand up or speak out in spite of our fear. When the right thing to do is to draw a line and stand behind it, and when we do that, the result is courage. Being afraid of the unknown is a normal human emotion, but if our fears rule our lives, then we will always experience the role of the victim. Or even worse, we will be used as a tool. Education in the form of free knowledge is powerful. Self-educated people choose their own curriculum. Their source of knowledge is fresh, unique, and not censored in any way... raw. Armed with such knowledge and with an open mind renders our fears obsolete.

Knowledge alone isn't power. But, putting the knowledge into play is where power comes from, and that takes courage. We all have this great human quality within us. Only a small group actually know how to tap its unlimited power. Courage is the gateway to life's hidden treasures. Sometimes all it takes is the courage to just be who you are.

Be Who You Are
There are some people that live their entire lives behind a mask. Living a life as someone other than your true self isn't living... it's hardly surviving.

I have a friend that recently came out and acknowledged herself as a woman. This shocked everyone she knew because my friend was born into the world in a male body. All of her physical features defined her as a man, except what she knew herself as from within.

To many in her circle, this came as a shock. Some even made life difficult for her because of their own refusal to accept the truth. I could see what this was doing to her spirit, as she would keep going back and forth on her decision, until finally she decided to hold her position and move forward as a woman. It took great courage to accept herself as who she knew herself to be from the inside.

I often think of how in-tune one has to be to recognize there is a problem when knowing that they were born into the wrong physical body. I had a hard time finding myself, and I came into the world with the right equipment issued. Many who don't understand it like I do say that My friend is sick, perverted, or confused. To them I say: Don't be quick to demonize what you don't understand. Try and think beyond your current position. Perspective is what shapes your reality. A higher perspective always comes with an advantage. Being capable of looking beyond your current field of vision only comes with gains. A better perspective will give you a cleaner picture and that is much more reliable than just an opinion.

Bruce Jenner was an Olympic decathlon winner. His accomplishment led to a career in film, television, writing, auto racing, and business. His fame even placed his picture on boxes of breakfast cereal. He lived most of his life in the public spotlight, but inside he was always a she. Finally, in 2015 Jenner came out as a trans woman.[23] Later that year she changed her name to Caitlyn. Some people were outraged when her actions of coming out and accepting herself as a woman was noted as an act of courage. There were even people that went as far as trying to demoralize her on social media channels. Throughout all of this, Caitlyn maintained her position and allowed her spirit to move forward.

---

23 Tony Duffy, "Caitlyn Jenner's transformation," CBS News, accessed August 3, 2017, http://www. cbsnews.com/pictures/bruce-jenner-over-the-years/.

Those who don't understand what these people are experiencing from within, try to demonize what they can't understand. Unfortunately for the weak and *closed-minded* thinker, they will never see past their own beliefs. It takes great courage to rise above the belief systems that are set up for everyone to follow. You have to know who you are first. Then, you must accept it. The courage comes when acceptance of who you are can no longer be denied.

For most of us, knowing who we are will only require some time away from the noise inside of our heads. Our true self is in there somewhere. Becoming the *who* that we are will take practice and lots of courage.

Making a Change

There are times when a huge change becomes necessary for survival. I can't think of a better example than being trapped in an abusive relationship. Domestic violence is one of the most volatile and dangerous situations a police officer can respond to. They are professionals that have the training to respond to dangerous situations. Imagine being the *untrained* victim.

Leaving an abusive relationship requires a lot of courage. This one action will set a whole new world into motion. I believe it's the idea of overwhelming change that keeps most abused spouses with their abusers. There are many factors that complicate the situation, and a simple picking up and leaving just won't work. For example, children make it difficult to leave. Although it's in their best interest to be removed from a toxic environment, the complexities of their daily lives do pose as a road block, and sometimes even a reason to stay.[24]

In some cases, the abuser may have cut off ties to a support network that the abused may have access to in order to leave. Many times, the abuser will control the finances and cripple the abused further by not having access to any money.

Emotions can also get in the way. Even after the abused spouse has successfully left the abuser behind, for one reason or another they end up

---

24   Kellie Holly, "Leaving an Abusive Relationship: Why Can't I Just Leave," Healthy Place, January 22, 2014, accessed August 7, 2017, https://www.healthyplace.com/blogs/verbala-buseinrelationships/2014/01/why-cant-i-leave-abuse/.

going right back into the abuser's arms. There is hope that the abuser will change, after promises are made by the abuser to that effect. Sometimes it takes several attempts until the abused gets the final "wake up call."

There are many other barriers that must be overcome in order to walk away from an abusive relationship. The risk of domestic violence homicide goes up upon separation, so the concern is very real and must be taken seriously. One thing is for certain: it takes tremendous courage to overcome an abusive relationship. Starting over is not easy, but in some cases very necessary.

If you feel you are trapped in an abusive relationship, there is hope for you. There are so many people like you that have found their freedom from that pit of darkness. You can have the same. There is a right way to go about it, and there is also a hard way. The first step is to contact an organization that can help. In the US, there is the National Domestic Violence Hotline.[25] You can start there and put together a safe exit strategy. The first step is picking up a phone and dialing the following numbers: 1-800-799- 7233.[26]

Daily Acts of Courage
Courage also comes in small doses, so if you need to stick a toe in the water before jumping right in, you can try some of these suggestions to get used to the idea.

- Engaging in an experience that is intimidating.
- Starting a conversation with a stranger.
- Asking someone on a date.
- Standing up for someone else or yourself.
- Catching a meal or a movie by yourself.
- Asking your boss for a raise.
- Making a list of your own fears and overcoming them head on.

25   Wiki how, "How to Leave an Abusive Relationship," last modified October 30, 2020, accessed March 23, 2021, http://www.wikihow.com/Leave-an-Abusive-Relationship.
26   National Domestic Violence Hotline, "Contact," accessed March 23, 2021, http://www. thehotline. org/about-us/contact/

These are just a few things that can get you used to the feeling of courage. The people who are noted throughout history are no different than you and me. The courage displayed by them in the darkest hours are what makes them who they are.

People like Martin Luther King Jr.[27] and Rosa Parks,[28] the Freedom Riders and all of those who put their lives in the line of harm to bring to life the Civil Rights Act of 1964.[29] This was a monumental achievement, and not just for one group of people, but for all people!

Mahatma Gandhi led his people against the British through nonviolent civil disobedience. What Gandhi did in India resulted in independence for his people and inspired freedom and civil rights across the world.[30] Civil disobedience is a powerful statement and sends shockwaves across the world. Think of policy so bad, the law-abiding public refuse to honor it into acceptance. I can't think of a more powerful message. And although harsh punishments can still be handed down, consistent civil disobedience will eventually send a loud and clear message to policy makers, that society will not tolerate such ideas or behaviors. This kind of power only comes with courage.

Emergency workers such as police officers, firemen and women, paramedics, and military personnel put their lives on the line daily in order to earn a living. These people risk their own lives to save ours. That is something that many take for granted, but more of us should admire and revel. I have a friend who was a combat medic during the Vietnam conflict. This guy jumped out of helicopters into hot zones to rescue injured Marines. His stories gave new meaning to the word courage. The most extreme scenario you could ever imagine, is what this Marine did every day for 3 years. I sometimes wonder how he managed to stay alive

27   4 MLA style, "Martin Luther King Jr. – Biography," Nobelprize.org. Nobel Media AB 2014, accessed August 29, 2017, http://www.nobelprize.org/nobel_prizes/peace/laure-ates/1964/king-bio.html.

28   Biography.com Editors, "Rosa Parks Biography.com," The Biography.com website, A&E Television Networks, last updated August 7, 2017, accessed August 29, 2017, https:// www.biography.com/people/rosa-parks-9433715.

29   Marian Smith Holmes, "The Freedom Riders Then and Now," Smithsonian.com, February 2009, accessed August 29, 2017, http://www.smithsonianmag.com/history/the-free- dom-riders-then-and-now-45351758/.

30   Biography.com Editors, "Mahatma Gandhi Biography.com," The Biography.com web-site, A&E Television Networks, last updated August 4, 2017, accessed August 29, 2017, https://www.biography.com/people/mahatma-gandhi-9305898.

to share his stories with me. Every day at work could have been his last. Almost any physical labor job requires courage to some degree.

Next time you see a tall building or a skyscraper, think of the people who wash the windows from the outside of those buildings. Then think of the iron workers who assembled that tall building. Roofers, landscapers, coal miners, tree trimmers, and anything else that involves the risk of injury or death on a daily basis all require courage. Many of these workers are taken for granted by the rest of society, and maybe even by themselves. Courage is something found in almost every action we take daily if we are conscious to it.

Uncommon Valor

Unbeknownst to us, we all possess the gift of courage to some degree. Though it may seem much safer to hide our heads in the sand more often, it is better for us to rise and stand for something. Unless we want to remain a prisoner to our own fears, moving forward into the great unknown will require us to tap into that courage.

The only way to know courage exists is to take that first step. Faith is what will see us through. In the moment of uncertainty, faith is the bridge we must walk onto in order to get to the next chapter in our lives. Faith is the knowing that whatever happens, we will be alright.

Every human on the planet has this gift of bravery somewhere within. Unfortunately, many of us choose not to use it, we ignore it, or even worse, we deny it. We admire the brave actions of the few who rise above their own fears to do amazing things, and even call them heroes or role models. These people aren't any different than any one of us. The gift of courage is only one of many powerful forces we have in our arsenal of life tools. It is up to the individual to discover it, get familiar with it, and apply it when needed to have a pleasant life experience.

Life's Toolbox

Sitting in a hole and complaining about how bad our life has become isn't going to make things any better. Especially when the tools you need are always with you. Courage is only one of the many tools we pick up along our journey through life. As human beings, we need to value the tools that make our lives easier and our experiences much more pleasant. The forces of nature are everywhere around our physical bodies.

These forces are always at work, even if we don't see, acknowledge, or believe in them. We have been given everything we need to navigate our way towards our desires. Now, all we have to do is learn to use the tools... and use them.

Chapter 7:
Use "The Force"

In 1977, film maker George Lucas, released Star Wars – A New Hope. This movie depicted incredible accomplishments when a small group of rebels rise up against an evil empire.[31] In this movie, there is talk of a great power called "the force" that allows those who can harness it to do amazing things like levitate and move large heavy objects, read and control the thoughts of others, and activate other super human powers. After seeing Star Wars, I was hooked. The thought of having such great power was beyond my imagination. I used to pretend that I had such great power. Although Star Wars was a science-fiction story, the concept of the force is very real.

According to the movie, there are two sides of this mysterious energy. There is a light side and a dark side, depending on how the force is to be used. Emotions of benevolence, compassion and mercy will yield the light side of the force. Those who use the light side are dedicated to live in harmony with the worlds around them. They were known as the Jedi. These warriors of peace used wisdom and logic over emotions and haste to draw their power from the force.

On the other hand, emotions of fear, resentment, and anger spun into hatred, malice, and rage toward all living things would draw out the dark side of the force. These dark overlords were known as the Sith. The Sith believed that the dark side of the force was much more powerful and it was also known to be more addictive.[32]

Lucas even went deeper into a detailed explanation of this energy field. There is the living force, which is connected to all living things and that connects all things together. Then there is the cosmic force, which is

---

31   Wikipedia, "Star Wars(film)," last modified March 13, 2018, https://en.wikipedia.org/ wiki/StarWars_ (film)
32   "The Force Explained - Star Wars 101," YouTube video, 5:38, posted by "Source Fed NERD," Oct 17,2015, https://www.youtube.com/watch?v=539SUcTrhDk.

everything that is living or that had lived together. Unifying force could be used to see into the future and the physical force could be used to levitate and move objects, no matter the size.

Science of the Force

From a perspective of science, everything is energy, and energy is always in motion. In the first Star Wars movie, Obi Wan Kenobi explains to Luke Skywalker that the force is an energy field that is created by all living things. It surrounds us, penetrates us, it binds the galaxy together. From there, the moviegoer is shown many examples of this science in full use.

Although you are only watching a science fiction movie, the great power that is displayed could *actually* be found within our own realm of reality. Humans do generate energy, so do animals and plants...even the earth generates energy, because it is a living thing too.

Sea of Energy

In 1899, physicist Nikola Tesla,[33] discovered that the earth receives, stores, and transmits energy. He believed that using different frequencies we could transmit information and power without wires to any part of the world. His goal was to harness the natural and renewable source of energy that exists between the earth and the ionosphere. Although he was not able to complete projects involving the wireless transmission of power, Tesla's work did result in the transmission of information, resulting in both AM and FM radio. Later, Tesla discovered Radiant Energy. It is not the nuclear energy as we have today. Radiant Energy is directly converted to electrical power by ionizing particles generated by radiant matter.

During the early 1930's, Thomas Henry Moray astonished witnesses with a demonstration of his Radiant Energy Power supply, that produced 50,000 watts of electricity.[34] More recently, a 13-year-old designed his own brand of free energy device. Inspired by Nikola Tesla and Albert

---

33   Therese Wade, "Nikola Tesla," Antara Healing Arts, March27, 2016, accessed August 7, 2017, https://antarahealingarts.com/tag/nikola-tesla.

34   Dr. Peter Lindemann, "T. Henry Moray," Free Energy, accessed August 7, 2017, http:// freeenergy. ws/t-henry-moray/.

Einstein, Max Loughan, a Nevada teenager, created his own energy device for less than $15.[35]

Using the Force in Real Life

The Force energy was based on true science, and if we are to understand life from behind the scenes, our mastery of it can make our lives easier and far more enjoyable than the struggles we face during any given day. So, science has proven that we are indeed living inside of an energy field – literally, a sea of energy surrounds every living life force. Even solid objects, like rocks are energy in motion. This was hard for me to grasp at first, but I do remember reading about material science in school a lifetime ago. The science behind water is a good example of this. When you freeze water, the energy slows down and it becomes ice (a solid). Heat up the ice and the energy will move faster; it turns back into a liquid. Boil water and the energy moves even faster and it turns into vapor.[36]

Everything in our world is relative to something else, and everything is energy. To master energy will take a lot of work and endless practice, but I do believe we have more power than we will ever know. In the movie Star Wars, Obi Wan Kenobi used a mind trick on a bar patron. In a later episode, Luke used that same Jedi mind trick to control the thoughts and actions of another character. The Jedi used this mind trick to avoid conflict. To the Jedi, combat was only in defense, and an absolute last resort. Using the Jedi Mind Trick can be done in real life if you know how to maintain your cool. Staying calm during a heated argument will always give you the upper hand. When a debate gets heated and tempers flare out, emotions take over and logic goes out the window. When you stay calm, you will always have a better chance to steer the conversation in a more favorable direction for you. Psychology is the Jedi Mind Trick, and it works.

When you find yourself in a situation that appears to be going sideways on you, remain calm and just use the force. You can be right or

---

35   Terence Newton, "13-Year-Old Invents Tesla Inspired Free Energy Device for Under $15," Waking Times, May 18, 2016, accessed August 7, 2017, http://www.wakingtimes.com/2016/05/18/13-year-old-invents-tesla-inspired-free-energy-device-for-under-15/.

36   Brad and Kate Silberberg, "What is Energy?" Mesa Creative Arts, accessed August 7, 2017, http://mesacreativearts.com/html/what_is_energy.html.

you can be happy. You always have a choice, and it is always yours to make. Just remember there is so much more you can learn about everything you think you already know. Like the Jedi, it will take a lifetime to become a master. Find a place to start and begin your training. Look for situations to apply your new-found wisdom, and, ***the force will be with you... always!***

Chapter 8:
Defeat

Defeat is a delightful feeling unless you find yourself on the wrong end. Being defeated isn't a very delightful experience. In fact, it could discourage one to press on, especially if it comes back-to-back. This would be a good time to reassess the plan and look for signs of weakness. There is always something that isn't in harmony that causes failure. Just because it's not visible at first glance doesn't mean that it's not present.

Sometimes you have to walk away and do something else for a while in order to reset your senses. This can be challenging when there is a time-sensitive matter. Unfortunately, the best things in life come in their own time. Haste will never yield quality, but sometimes *good enough* will have to work. The way we look at the situations we find ourselves in, and the way we allow those situations to affect us, creates the experience. If we are able to justify a loss as a win in the mind, our outlook will point more towards a win rather than defeat.

The Perception

As a perfectionist, this idea of good enough has always caused tension, because in my mind, having to settle for less than perfect equated to defeat. I am one who believes in the value of quality over quantity. I follow this mindset in almost everything I do. Most of my adult life, I have been fortunate enough to be my own boss. Self-employment has allowed me to take the time I need to make sure what I am doing is done correctly the first time.

Working for others, I don't always have the luxury of time. Everyone wants the best quality and the most production, even if a little quality is compromised. Sometimes *good enough* will have to work. Operating under the production mentality, that's the standard. Defeat in this case isn't failure, but a victory. Today, I don't use the word defeat in my vocabulary. Instead, I use *set back* and victory.

Never Take It Too Seriously

Over the years, I've learned to let go of things that cause tension and grief. I am still a work-in-progress, but it's getting easier to let go of things outside of my control. Taking everything so seriously makes it hard to enjoy life. I have to keep in mind the importance of experience over whatever it is that I am fixated on.

I have found that the more relaxed and calm I am going into a project, the smoother and enjoyable the whole experience becomes. Work doesn't seem like work, and the days fly like the wind into the sails of a ship.

Loving what you do is very important when it comes to success. Sure, you can be successful doing something you hate, but *why* put that much effort into something you hate? Besides, with passion behind what you do, the journey becomes enjoyable. After all, who doesn't want to be happy? Happiness is only a state of mind. Happiness is also subjective from individual to individual, and there are many paths to it for each player. Think of life as a game. To win the game, you must always first learn the rules... and just don't quit.

Winners Never Quit; Quitters Never Win

There is a big difference between failure and quitting. It has been said that to win, one must know how to fail. Failure is part of the learning process. Failing is necessary to learn and master, because from there you can only rise. You can try over and over until you win. When you quit, you are done. Failure has never stopped massively successful people from reaching their level of greatness. In fact, most, if not all, successful people have failed at some point in their early careers.[37]

A teacher once told **Thomas Edison** that he was *"too stupid"* to learn anything. Edison went on to become one of the most inspirational

---

37   Richard Feloni and Ashley Lutz, "23 Incredibly Successful People Who Failed at First," Business Insider, March 7, 2014, accessed August 7, 2017, http://www.businessinsider. com/successfulpeople-who-failed-at-first-2014-3/#nston-churchill-was-estranged- from-his-political-party-overideological-disagreements-during-the-wilderness-years- of-1929-to-1939-1.

world figures in history. Thomas Edison created some of the most widely used products the world had ever seen. Some of his innovations include the incandescent electric light bulb, the telegraph, the kinetograph (early camera for shooting motion pictures), the universal stock ticker, and the phonograph, among other things. He held more than one thousand patents.[38] Edison believed that if you failed enough times, a sure-win was just ahead.

Walt Disney was fired from a newspaper that said he *"lacked imagination and had no original ideas."* In 1923, Disney opened a Hollywood studio. Within 5 years, his studio created "Steamboat Willie" which went on to become the iconic Mickey Mouse. In 1934, Disney began work on Snow White and the Seven Dwarfs. During the 1940's, Disney had released a treasure chest full of American cartoon classics such as Pinocchio, Dumbo, Fantasia, and Bambi. By 1950, Disney had released its first live action film. In July of 1955, he opened Disneyland, the most popular theme park in the world. Although he died in 1966, his company moved on to continue his legacy. In 1971, **Walt Disney World Resort** opened in Bay Lake and Lake Buena Vista, Florida, near Orlando.[39] Today, Walt Disney is a multi-billion-dollar empire. All of this was the creation of someone who believed in his dreams and took the necessary steps to make it a reality. Failure helped this one man find his way to epic success!

Michael Jordan was cut from a high school basketball team. Today, he is one of the seven greatest players ever. From the mid-1980s to the late 1990s, Michael Jordan dominated basketball. He led the Chicago Bulls to six NBA championships and earned the National Basketball Association Most Valuable Player Award five times. Michael Jordan became the most

---

38   Biography.com Editors, "Thomas Edison Biography," The Biography.com, A&E Television Networks, last updated August 4, 2017, accessed August 7, 2017, https://www.biography.com/people/thomas-edison-9284349.

39   Biography.com Editors, "Walt Disney Biography," The Biography.com, A&E Television Networks, last updated August 7, 2017, accessed August 7, 2017, https://www.biography. com/people/walt-disney-9275533.

decorated player in the NBA. His net worth is estimated to be over $1 billion. His secret for success? *Always try to outdo yourself.*[40]

Converting Defeat into a Priceless Asset

To convert a defeat into a win, you must see the failure as a sign that your plan needs mending. While the feeling of loss may be unpleasant in the moment, the defeat is *actually* beneficial. It serves as a warning that an error in calculation or judgement is present. Every negative emotion can be transformed into a constructive power. ***Self-discipline*** allows one to change unpleasant emotion into a driving power. The more one practices self-discipline, the stronger the will becomes, and the easier it becomes to push through the next crisis.

Another thing to consider are the effects this can have on the *subconscious mind*. Since the subconscious mind accepts and acts on one's mental attitude, the more defeat is looked at as everlasting rather than a mild set-back, the subconscious mind will eventually accept defeat as being permanent. Keep in mind, the subconscious cannot tell the difference between reality and fiction. With having such an advantage, why would we consciously place ourselves at a disadvantage by thinking our way out of a great position?

This sounds perplexing, but I assure you there is a rational explanation behind this phenomenon. Just because we can't draw any connections between negative energies and our negative experiences, doesn't mean that there isn't one there...or rule out what we are missing. We have a choice to make. Either we learn from our mistakes, learn from others, or continue to make the same mistakes over and over again.

Defeat can either become an asset or a liability, depending on how it is programmed into the subconscious mind. We will be going over self-discipline and programming the subconscious mind in later chapters of this book. But for now, take note of ***how much power*** you can gain or give away by making one simple choice.

---

40   Biography.com Editors, "Michael Jordan Biography," The Biography.com, A&E Television Networks, last updated August 1, 2017, accessed August 7, 2017, https://www.biography.com/people/michael-jordan-9358066.

Fuel for Self-Determination

Success consciousness requires one to let go of failure consciousness. When we hold on to failures of our past instead of looking toward where we want to be, and taking the necessary actions to get there, we bring defeat onto our self. By using the data, we get from analyzing our mistakes, we can move closer into a winning position. Mistakes are only building blocks of character and the fuel for self-determination.

Another facet of determination is a physical handicap or sudden loss of one or more of the five senses. Ludwig Van Beethoven's deafness didn't stop him from becoming one of the world's most renown musicians. He wrote some of his best work when he was almost completely deaf.[41]

Stevie Wonder was born six weeks premature, and as a result of too much oxygen pumped into his incubator, he was left permanently blind. Stevie's blindness didn't stop him from becoming the youngest solo artist to have a number one R&B song on the Billboard Top 100.[42] Some may conclude that the loss of one or more of the five senses, tends to push someone that is determined for success even harder for it. In the cases of Ludwig Van Beethoven and Stevie Wonder, I would have to agree with that conclusion.

---

41   Biography.com Editors, "Ludwig van Beethoven Biography," The Biography.com, A&E Television Networks, last updated April 27, 2017, accessed August 7, 2017, https://www. biography.com/people/ludwig-van-beethoven-9204862.

42   Kendall Deflin, "10 Things You Never Knew About Stevie Wonder," Live for Live Music, May 13, 2017, accessed August 7, 2017, http://liveforlivemusic.com/features/10- things-stevie-wonder/.

Chapter 9:
Self-Discipline

Without self-discipline or self-control, success will remain a dream. As human beings, we are gifted with free will. This means we can think and do anything we want... *but not without consequence.* To achieve our greatest potential, we will need to have some kind of order, and that will require discipline.

Life and Death: My Personal Experience

Practicing self-discipline has become my latest point of focus. Among other things in my life that need order, my health is also in jeopardy without proper structure and discipline. I have been overweight most of my adult life. I'm not proud of my bad eating habits, but I have been cleaning up my act. My focus has been more on spirit and mind in the last decade or so. But now, I need to bring my body into the balancing act... if I want to keep this game going on a while longer.

Several years ago, I was diagnosed with type 2 diabetes. At first, I was in denial about it. Then, I became angry at myself for allowing it to happen. Some days are better than others, but I do feel the effects of the diabetes, and I cannot ignore the effects any longer. I go for regular checkups and my blood is tested every few months. Just to be safe, I had my heart checked out and had a few stress tests done in the last several years.

Now, I check my blood sugar more often and watch what I eat. Doing this has brought some improvement to my life, but getting my weight in check is still a struggle. Education, a consistent diet and exercise program, and a commitment towards a goal has proven to work for those that found success before me. This seems like a good place to start. Goals are good, but only if they are realistic and obtainable. My mind must also be in the game. Otherwise, I will battle myself into a mudhole. I've created enough of those situations for myself in the past. I don't need to create another one. Playing the recordings of those events in my mind is effective enough to get the point.

To get the results I want, there must be action in the direction of those results. This is my latest hole. I seem to be stuck, but all is not lost. Some days, I have no energy to move. When the fatigue is too much to tolerate, I must push myself beyond my own limits. If the disease wins, I lose my life... and I'm not done with this one yet. I don't fight Diabetes. It will kick my ass... as it always has, and it will continue to whip me relentlessly, and without mercy. No, I don't battle diabetes. I *respect* it. It is worth my time, to learn more about it, so I can manage it as best as I can. I don't fight grizzly bears either. One of those could do as much damage to me as the diabetes in merely a few seconds!

It's important to remember that every thought and action comes with consequence. The golden key to success in life is discipline. Because, anything of value requires your commitment to master. Without self-discipline, there is nothing there to bind an idea to the commitment that is required to transform the idea into a physical manifestation. So far, I'm not seeing any improvement using medication. So, my next move is to find a better alternative to this condition that has its grip on every part of my body. Whatever I find that will help me overcome this disorder will require discipline to restore my body back to health.

The Key to Success in Life

Self-discipline is not only the key to good health, but to succeed in any part of life, the formula for success is the same. There are those among us that seem to have the magic with them. Everything they do and everything they touch turns to *gold*, and they make it look so easy and effortless. These people aren't magicians, wizards or witches. They have found a system that works, and they are committed to it.

A key is usually required to access anything of value. There are many keys to living and enjoying life. So many of us only survive, but to live we need to do a little work. I'm not talking about the kind of work you do at your job every day. I'm talking about doing something to better your life. There are keys that will open opportunities that you never thought existed, and all you have to do is look for them. It has been said that the best things in life are free! There is truth to that statement. *Self-discipline* is one of those keys to opportunity, but there are other keys to self-discipline as well.

Sense of Purpose

Having a sense of purpose is very important if you are seeking self-discipline. Without a sense of purpose, it is impossible to make a commitment to anything. There are a lot of people today that are afraid of commitment. They drift through life always searching and never finding. They are like a ship without a destination, a rudder, or a crew. These people start projects but never finish them, change jobs frequently and are in and out of relationships. They never stay involved with anything long enough to be successful at it. "*Leaving your options open*" will only commit you to failure. Without a sense of purpose, you can't apply yourself to any one thing, and without applying yourself to something you can't succeed.

Thirst for Knowledge

Education is also very important. I'm not talking about going back to school. We live in the era of information. Every household has access to the information pipeline. Kids now have cell phones that can access the internet from anywhere they go... so do the adults. We all have the ability to learn. Unfortunately, many of us are too *lazy* to do the work, and some are too stubborn to let go of beliefs that have been failing consistently. ***We seem to be drowning in information and starving for knowledge.*** Being open to new ideas and trying new things will open doors to new opportunities. If you feel like you are stuck or trapped, try something new. It has been said: *Nothing changes if nothing changes*. Everything around you will change, but if you are indecisive or inactive, your situation may not change for the better.

Self-Assurance

Well-disciplined people are eager to learn and not married to any one method of getting things done. They never lose sight of their goals but are open to other ways of achieving them. This requires an open mind and willingness. I call it the *"Whatever It Takes"* attitude. Ruminating over past failures will only start a vicious cycle of negative reinforcement that results in a fear of more failure.

Once you say I can't, you have already decided that you *won't*. Those who are self-disciplined, display self-assurance that can't be shaken. Their confidence is strong and even if they fail, their attitude toward failure isn't negative at all. Their point of view is that they are just another step closer to a victory. The optimist is self-confident, but the pessimist is riddled in self-doubt. This negative way of thinking is what creates their negative experience. They get to prove themselves right once again. If you find yourself loathing this negative mentality, ask yourself: **Do I want to be right or do I want to be happy?**

Sensory Vision

People who are well-disciplined have sensory vision. They can visualize what they want in full detail. This skill comes from having a strong imagination. You may think that imagining things are for kids, or that you don't have a creative bone in your body. Believe me, you do. We all have the ability to imagine and create. Some of us use this skill more than others, but we are all capable... *even you*. Once you set your goal, visualize the results in clear sensory-rich detail. Imagine the rewards of success in sight, sound, taste, touch, and even smell. Always keep this vision with you and revisit it often.

Organized Structure

Some things require more than one phase to complete. I remember a time when a huge project was presented to me. My first thought was to turn and run! I was overwhelmed by the amount of work, the number of details, and the short deadlines. My friend turned to me and said:

"We don't have to eat the whole elephant in one bite, we can break it down into nibbles." This, by the way, is a creative way to visualize a solution to a problem. Of course, we weren't going to eat an actual elephant, but *the idea* of consuming an animal that large in one bite drove his point clear into my mind.

Planning and organization skills are helpful when a job has to be pieced together in phases. Setting priorities from the most important to the least important, and sequencing things to be done in a specific order, will simplify any task too big for one bite. This is how most factories operate. Assembly lines are staffed with employees that focus on one thing, then as the product passes from one area to the next, it is assembled in the correct order. Any task can be set up this way. All that is needed is to set the right order in the process, then follow it through. The book you are reading went through such a process.

Perseverance

This is one very important ingredient to the success recipe. Having a dream and setting goals are a great start, but without resolve nothing will get done. Disciplined achievers are tenacious in their resolve. They *actually* enjoy the work and the process. Those who lack discipline will quit when the job becomes too difficult, uncomfortable, or just too much to handle. Perseverance is a unique quality that will place you in the upper 10% of aggressive achievers.

I see too many young people that are so fragile that they will walk off from a jobsite because their feelings were injured. So many more refuse to show up for work because of a runny nose, an ingrown toenail, or rain. These are the same people who do the bare minimum at their job, waste company time on their phones instead of doing what they are being paid for, and complain about their rate of pay. Getting through to them is impossible because they lack a sense of *purpose*. All they can comprehend is: *"Why am I not making enough money?"* They are stuck in a hole that just keeps getting deeper as time goes on. Sadly, what they are missing is that more money only comes as a result of showing what you are worth, first. If you are selling yourself to a potential employer, you need to become aware of a few things:

1. merely saying you are worth what you think you deserve, and being able to demand such compensation, are at opposite ends of the galaxy!
2. You are talking to someone who has heard the same line of b.s. from everyone walking in his/her doors looking for an opportunity.
3. The person you are trying to convince with words, has witnessed people's actions on countless occasions. Sitting through another session with you isn't going to be interesting or desirable, unless you have something really unique.

A Personal Experience

Being self-employed, I have found situations where my life seems to be out of control. When I used to work for others, I did my job, punched a clock and left work at work. But now, I can't just leave work, because my office is at home. This blurs the line between work and home. Often, an idea will force me back in front of my computer in the middle of the night. I do this because great ideas don't appear on demand, and if I don't take advantage of the opportunity, it will be gone forever. It's perseverance that keeps me working, sometimes even into the night. Ultimately, this is what is needed to create and maintain a successful business.

Perseverance is the fuel for a success-driven individual. To be success-driven requires more than a pipe dream. It involves actual work. Those who keep jumping from job to job, looking for better pay, are not success-driven. They are wasting the most valuable commodity on this planet, and in this life existence... time.

Patience

Time is not your enemy. Everyone thinks that the world revolves around time. *Actually*, it's the opposite. Time is the measurement of movement of the earth in space. Time isn't money; you can't print it. And time isn't something you can stretch or shrink.

If you are focused on a goal, and your goal is to do the best job you can, time cannot be your focus. You cannot manage time, but you can manage you. The best way to save time is to not waste it. Worrying about time is wasting it. Having to do something over again to correct it doesn't save time (or money). It has been said that patience is a virtue. It truly is. If you ask for patience, you will find yourself in many situations where you can practice it. So be careful for what you ask for. You will more likely get it in a form you weren't expecting.

Self-Control in Society

We live in a diverse world. There are over eight *billion* people walking the earth, and the number continues to grow. In our country alone, there are people from all parts of the planet, each with their own culture, religion, ideas, and opinions. We can all get along with each other, if we make a few adjustments to our own thoughts and behaviors. While we don't have direct control of what others think, say, and do, we can control ourselves. By doing so, we do have some indirect control on the overall outcome, to some degree. Finding our self in a heated debate with another person or a group of people won't end well if our choice of action is to spew hate rhetoric. Dumping gasoline on a raging fire will only intensify the inferno. The same will happen here. I see this happening more often these days than ever before.

A Society Out of Control

In diverse societies, people will sometimes take to the streets, and even during what starts out as a peaceful protest, always seems to end with people going to jail. Some people think they will get their point across more successfully by blocking traffic. These scenarios usually end with someone in the hospital or in the morgue. Then, video and pictures surface on social media sites resulting in even more hatred and anger. All of this goes on and nobody ever stops to think about their *own* part in the madness. Sitting quietly and doing nothing is a choice. Turning a blind eye to known evil is also a choice. Supporting such known evil is also a choice. It seems like nobody sees their part in this grand creation we are all a part of, happening in *real time*.

We are a society that is spinning out of control, and it's getting *worse*. Nobody wants to claim their part for the demise of our world, because we have distanced ourselves from responsibility. People are all great at pointing fingers. We say things like: *"it's Obama's fault,"* and *"Donald Trump is ruining our country!"* We continue to do this over and over, giving in to further chaos. But, one thing we never consider is: *What is MY part in this?*

Although we may feel that what we are doing is righteous, our mind is hijacked by the *ego* as we sit at our computers and phones spreading hate-fueled propaganda. We blast those who see the current situation from a different perspective without any further investigation on our part.

It's so easy to see why our society is out of control when we are so easily led to believe whatever we are told to think. Our society is out of control because we refuse to think critically for ourselves. Critical thinkers cannot be manipulated because they think by way of logic.

Some Hope Is Still Left

Those at the top work in the dark. They use mind control to keep people conditioned to the programming. By doing so, they've managed to keep their positions secure for a very long time. People are starting to wake up and shake off the programming and you can see it in 2023. What you see on mainstream has changed. There is still a lot of censorship still going on. But there is still a lot of content being shared among the population that shows a change in social condition on many platforms. People are beginning to see beyond the indoctrination programs.

What can I Do?

You may think *"I'm only one person, I can't change the world."* **Martin Luther King Jr.** was only one person, and he *did* change the world. He started a movement so powerful it inspired people of all ethnicity to get involved in a campaign for human rights. **John F. Kennedy** was only one person, and he saved the world from nuclear annihilation. It doesn't take much more than changing your own thoughts and actions to get others to do the same. People generally follow the actions of others. I know we like to believe we are unique and sophisticated individuals, but sadly we aren't. If we were, we wouldn't be so easy to control. However, we do have free will, and we do exercise it. We can choose to be the way we are now, or to change our ways. Our thoughts are the most powerful force in the universe. If we all learn to harness that power, the world will change. It only takes a few adjustments and a lot of practice. I know this sounds too easy, but most things are.

My Experience

I used to think writing a book was impossible for me to do. Here I am writing my fifth book. I started writing my first book in 2007, then I wrote my second one in 2010. Neither one made it to print because I didn't feel either book was worthy to invest in. I went back to researching and writing. This went on for years. In 2016, I released my first nonfiction book: *Higher Powered: A Book of Powerful Secrets to Finding Happiness*. Then, in 2017, I released the second part to that first book: *Highest Self: A Book of Powerful Secrets to Leash the Ego*. With each book I write, I get to learn more about life and my part in it. I get to test my new-found knowledge. And best of all, I get to share this wisdom with the rest of the world.

Will my books change the world? The material in them sure has the potential. I didn't rush to get something into print. I did lots of research and invested a great deal of time and money to have them edited by professionals. The result was a quality product that I was proud to put my name on. I did this by pursuing the steps that a well-disciplined achiever would follow.

I still find myself in a hole from time to time, but I have lots of tools to get out whenever I want. The amount of time I spend in a hole is always up to me. Lately, I haven't been wasting too much of my time on my back, looking up at the surface of the ground above. But there are days when shamelessly... I do!

The Benefits of Self Discipline

Those who lack self-discipline will struggle a lot in life. I say this from *my own* experience. Self-discipline has been the most difficult tool to master. I know what I am to become. I can also visualize myself in the role. But, some days the defects of the *human* condition all gang up and really kick my ass! Going against all odds is a level of *faith* not many people have in their own abilities. It is sad to think, but true. In the moment of weakness, I have to *push* myself beyond where *my mind* says is the end. In a world that seems like there is no end to struggle, keeping my cool is most important. To use logic, calm is the perfect state of mind to be in. To get something programmed into memory also requires repetitive practice.

There are always going to be people who test the limits of my patience. Most of the time it's when I am in traffic. I am most vulnerable to losing my cool when I am driving, especially when another driver puts my life at risk to save a few minutes from his/ her commute. I need to remind myself that it isn't worth giving away my day to an ignorant human that has no idea what he/ she is doing, or how his/ her actions affect other people. I remember installing train horns on my truck. I used to honk, roll my window down to curse and give obscene finger signals to offensive drivers. Now, I am much calmer. I follow a simple set of rules that instantly restore my serenity. Nobody has the power to set me off unless I give them that power. Here are the rules:

Maintaining self-control in an argument
- Keep cool when others get hot.
- Treat everyone with respect.
- Never engage in conversation when angry.
- There are three sides to every argument.
- Practice asking questions and listening to the answers.
- Don't say or do anything that will hurt another.

- Look for something positive in every unpleasant situation

These rules have kept me out of fights, out of trouble, and out of jail. People do not know how to react to this kind behavior. Their first instinct is to become aggressive, but when I trip them up with compassion, understanding and love, they become confused. The moment when they realize I am not going to participate in conflict is priceless.

Sometimes they get even more heated, and then once their hot air is all used up, there is only silence. I will give them the floor and let them vent every insult until there is nothing left. Then, I have everything I need to find common ground. I will slay them with kindness and understanding. More often, they will feel embarrassed about their behavior and apologize. But sometimes their initial intent was to ridicule and insult with malice. Those are the ones I pray for. There must be some form of pain lingering in their heart, or at least that is what I sell to myself. This works more effectively when you understand the workings of the subconscious mind.

Being calm when others are heated gives you the upper hand and you will have full control of the conversation immediately. It takes incredible strength to maintain your cool during conflict. Most people don't have that much self-control. In fact, most people run only on raw emotion, and they don't know that they are being led through the entire conversation at all.

Self-discipline is a life tool worth learning how to use in the human experience. It has helped me achieve some very amazing things, and every time I utilize this marvelous tool, my life becomes better and my experiences are always more pleasant.

SECTION 3

The Subconscious Mind

Chapter 10:
The Mind and its Mysteries

The mind is an incredible piece of machinery. Although it is non- physical, it's powers go beyond human understanding. People often mistake it for the brain, but it's not the brain. The brain is flesh, and therefore a part of the physical body. The mind is non-physical and controls the brain and every other part of the body, to sustain life and do its bidding. The best analogy would be looking at **the brain** as hardware, and **the mind** as the *software* and *virtual* hard drive. The potential power of the human mind transcends words and quite literally... *your wildest dreams*!

You have no idea of the infinite power and possibilities that lies sleeping within you. That's why I say: "***You have more power than you will ever know.***" An awakened mind is in a constant process of unfolding. Like the petals of a flower, it continues to unfold and reveal *more* hidden truths and treasures, as long as we're ready to accept more.

A mind that keeps working towards further development will develop more powers of comprehension. As of now, It's the great creation center that's running on auto-pilot, waiting for you to discover it. People often *misuse* it because they aren't aware of what it is. Most people won't go out of their way to learn about this amazing and *powerful tool*.

THIS BOOK WAS WRITTEN FOR THE SOLE PURPOSE OF DEFINING THE MIND AND ITS POWERS. *If you can master this remarkable tool, you will ultimately master every area of your life all at once!* Although humankind hasn't completely understood the mind's full potential, the scientific community has been studying its mysteries for many years, and found great things take place behind its curtains. Anything becomes possible or impossible within the limits we set in the mind. We do know that there are two sides of the mind, and some sources even mention a third.[43]

The Thinking Mind

The conscious mind is also the thinking mind, but don't confuse mental activity with *thinking*. The thought process is almost completely left out of the decision-making equation these days. Most people do not think. Have you observed the way people behave lately? They wouldn't behave this way if they were thinking. Would you consider acting like a fool, thoughtful behavior? Listen to what people say. Most of it isn't done by applying *thought* to it.

Thinking is a skill that can be picked up as easily as *typing* or *playing the guitar*. Unfortunately, there are no courses offered that teach **effective thinking**. It's up to us as individuals to seek out better ways of thinking.

Being *self-taught*, I never had limits or boundaries to the curriculum of my education. I had access to knowledge that is limited to only those who go beyond the scope of **traditional education**. My process of thinking adapted to the *limitless* environment I created. Those who discount the true value of self-education, and only view a formal degree as credentials of knowledge, are missing the bigger picture. There is a lot of *free* knowledge out there for you to find and apply. **Hidden knowledge** is only for those who seek it and will dig to find it. Most often it is hidden right in front of you! This goes back to winning at the game of life. Knowing more will always give you the player's advantage. Your *thoughts* are where the process of creation begins. This is a *powerful* tool worth knowing about!

To get a better understanding of the power of our thoughts, we need to understand **the mind** better. Since most of us don't look past the surface for answers, and even more don't even bother to ask *any questions*, it's very clear why we find ourselves in a hole.

The mind is the creation center of our life. Thoughts are the first step to any creation. Since everything is energy, your thought energy when mixed with emotions will raise or lower your vibrational frequency

---

43   "The Trinity of Mind –The Conscious, Subconscious, and Unconscious." YouTube video, 8:39. Posted by "The Event Is coming soon." February 10, 2017. https://www.youtube. com/watch?v=aw600ullhQ4.

(*from an atomic level*). Then, the **subconscious mind** picks up on that energy frequency and starts the process of creating something to fit that frequency. Think of it like tuning in a radio station. In between stations are static noises. If you want to hear your favorite music, you MUST tune in! As we learn more about how the conscious mind and subconscious mind work together, we can utilize the mind and its incredible powers to better our lives.

Conscious and Subconscious Mind

The **conscious mind** involves the *objective* world and awareness. It processes incoming data in real time using the five senses. Although it has no memory and processes only one thing or one event at a time, it can tap into the **subconscious mind** for what it lacks and needs. Habits are set by training the subconscious mind through the conscious mind... sort of like programming. In other words, you can access the subconscious side through the conscious side of the mind. The conscious mind is also in charge of making decisions, so it can reject an idea if it deems it *not true*. But once an idea passes through to the subconscious mind, the idea cannot be rejected, but can be *overwritten* with another program in the form of *new information*. Additional data can change the overall picture, and *usually* does.

The conscious mind only holds onto things that are in a constant state of change. Repetition *tires* the conscious mind and it will send anything that repeats to the subconscious side to store as a program. Practice something over and over and you will find it becomes easier to do over time. This is because it has become a memory now. Learning misinformation as being fact is also achieved by repetition, and stored as memory.

Practice Makes It Perfect

I remember picking up the guitar for the first time. Placing my fingers on the fretboard to form chords seemed awkward and very uncomfortable at first. Changing finger positions was even harder. Then, I had to pick certain strings and skip others while changing finger positions. As if all of this wasn't hard enough, it had to be done in proper timing.

Playing music is like the inner workings of a clock. Everything must be precise and in perfect sequence for it to work. I practiced my guitar for hours every day for years before I could be "musically fluent" enough to play a live show, or go into a professional studio to record (without costing me a fortune)! Today, after years of not playing, I can pick up my guitar and play a few hours and be ready for a live performance, or a studio session. This is because my mind has all the songs programmed into it already. If you wonder how a musician can remember so much music to do a live performance, this is the subconscious mind taking over. In fact, it usually takes only a few notes to start the entire program.

Subconscious Mind

The subconscious mind is beneath awareness and is the subjective world. It is here, where we create who we think we are. Emotions, memories, and beliefs are all kept here in the subconscious mind, along with all of the programs that control our thoughts and behaviors. In addition to being a storage device, it also acts as a decoding device that decodes the imagination, feelings, sensations, impulses, and instincts, which produce intuition.

The subconscious mind also controls all our body functions as well. This side of the mind is a world of chaos that works to precision, like the inner workings of a clock. The subconscious mind will take your thoughts very literally and turn them into experience. This is why you want to be very careful of the thoughts you send into the subconscious, because it will create your experience exactly on the root focus of those thoughts. It's been said that thoughts become things. This happens when emotions mix with thought. To create your physical reality, you form your subjective reality, and set your perspective on how you view the world.

So, if we want to change a thought pattern or a behavior, it has to start here, in the subconscious. When we change our subjective views, we create a much different experience. Because we are limited only to our perception, our experiences also become limited. To expand our experiences, we must expand our perception.

Unfortunately, this expansion can occur on its own, in any direction, if we don't grab the wheel and steer it. Allowing the subconscious mind to steer itself is the reason why most of the earth's population lives in poverty. To do more than merely survive, you must be willing to take control and steer your own ship consciously. Those programs within the subconscious mind can be overwritten, but it takes awareness, effort, and lots of practice to change them.

Unconscious Mind

The unconscious mind is the universe and all the laws of nature beneath the chaos. It's the objective world, the afterlife, and is highly structured and organized. It's everything we don't understand about life, and it connects us to the collective consciousness. The unconscious mind is about nature, the universal mind, and the governing patterns of life.

My understanding is that this is what people refer to as the soul or spirit. As humans, we try to complicate everything for some reason (not yet determined). Making things simple to understand would be just too easy for us to accept. In my research of the different parts of the mind, I found mostly two sides. I am only guessing this third side is to explain the regions of the mind to those who don't believe in *the word* "spirit."

Power of Words Over Experience

In my books, I keep it as simple to understand as possible. You can call something whatever you like... call it a *bologna sandwich* if it makes you happy. Just know what it is. Spirit is energy. That's it, just pure energy. Even those who denounce God and religion can agree with this much science. I have gone on to explain that energy cannot be created or destroyed, and almost all intelligent people will agree.

It seems that the language is what trips people up. Everyone has their own understanding of what a word means. People rely on words so much that they allow their mind to play "gatekeeper." Instead of focusing their mind on the meaning of the message, most people rely on the meaning of the word. For this reason alone, we are lost to who and what we are. Our beliefs and patterns of behavior are programmed before we are old enough to agree or disagree with them.

As children, we are natural explorers of the universe. Our minds soak up everything we are told, as well as what we discover on our own. For some reason, we seem to hang on more to what we are told than what we experience. This is the "conditioning" process that guides our thinking patterns and molds our beliefs. If we were more aware of the programs running in the background, I'm sure we would have made the necessary adjustments to our thinking process to better suit our own needs. As a result of our hubris, we have dug ourselves in so deep, that a completely new mindset is required for us to ever be free again!

In 2020, words like "social distancing" and "new normal" began to appear in conversations in the mainstream. What is normal about anything that occurred in 2020? How is distancing yourself from others social behavior? See the conflict in terms? This is social engineering in play. Psychologically, you are being programmed to accept this behavior through consistent repetition. Same as learning a new skill like typing or playing a guitar... everything that goes in is stored, but that which repeats over and over becomes a command, and then a recorded program.

"If you tell a lie big enough and keep repeating it, people will eventually come to believe it. The lie can be maintained only for such time as the State can shield the people from the political, economic and/or military consequences of the lie. It thus becomes vitally important for the State to use all of its powers to repress dissent, for the truth is the mortal enemy of the lie, and thus by extension, the truth is the greatest enemy of the State."

- Joseph Goebbels
(Reich Minister of Propaganda 1933 - 1945)

It's hard to believe that our complex minds will allow the most ridiculous nonsense and accept it as fact. Unfortunately, it will, and there are no limits to what the mind will or will not believe. This is what is meant by free will. We are free to believe in whatever we want. Religion teaches that the creator gifted mankind free will. And although there are some truths found in all religions, they're mostly hidden among tales of wild fiction. In order to uncover the truths, we must rely on our intuition as our guide, and remember that our experience and our feelings about them override the lesser form of communication we call "words." In other words, always go with your gut feeling first!

Prisoner of Your Own Beliefs

Those of us that can't shake off the programmed belief systems are going to remain in a state of limbo until they do. As a human being, we are meant to use these bodies to explore who we are as individuals. Our minds have the ability to change perspective. By changing perspective, we change the outcome experience, and we evolve. The longer we hang on to the same perspective, the more our experience will seem to resemble that of living in a prison.

Beliefs are nothing more than outdated programs. It's only the value we place on them that gives them the power to control us. Really, the only difference between the most amazing people on the planet and everyone else is what they believe. Amazing people don't set limitations on themselves. They let their spirit drive their minds. By using the power of belief, one can change the outcome and experience of any situation life will throw at them.

Belief is also a natural law, so managing your thinking is critical! The mechanics behind this law have been outlined above, and they are very simple and easy to understand. The things we think and say over and over on the conscious side, become written as programs on the subconscious side. Eventually, we find ourselves behind walls we constructed with dead ideas and broken dreams... a virtual prison of our own making.

Maintaining an open mind will bring down the walls around it. Until we can open our mind to a different belief, we remain imprisoned in it. We must never forget that our beliefs have the power to keep us in a hole or give us the power to move mountains... and that is always our choice to make.

When Escape Becomes Necessary

Faith in the context of progress is an essential ingredient to success. However, there are times when it's better to let go than continuing to embrace something holding us back. It's important to remember that our mind stores and controls everything we think, say, and do. The time to change our mind is when our experience becomes a constant negative flow of energy. When we feel tension or resistance to something, that is a sure sign of turbulent energy. If we choose to ignore these warning signs, the results aren't going to be favorable ones.

Life is full of wonders and hidden treasures. To gain access to these rewards, we must escape our current beliefs, if it no longer serves us. The willingness to let go of past ideas will put a new way of thinking into motion. We bounce back into positive energy motion like a light switch just flipped on. The delay from negative to positive thinking is only in the time it takes us to escape our failed past beliefs. Viewing our beliefs as a game plan rather than pre-determined destiny will give us flexibility. The more we can hone into something closer to what we want, the faster we will achieve it.

Rigidness in planning is foolish. Things happen along the way that could change the outcome from good to bad. If you follow a rigid plan, you will put yourself in another hole. Life isn't scripted...ever! If you leave out this important detail, expect failure. There should always be flexibility in planning so that the objective becomes the focus, and not the steps leading to the objective. In other words, the objective doesn't change, but *the plan* might have to.

A Paradigm Shift Is Needed

A paradigm is like a *blueprint* that we use to build our lives. In science and philosophy, paradigm is a set of concepts, theories or thought patterns that becomes the framework for proof. Even easier to understand, a paradigm is a mental program that has complete control over our habitual behavior. Change is a fact of life. Everything is in a constant state of motion. Although change is uncomfortable for a lot of us, it is what it is, and we must overcome our fear of it.

A paradigm shift is needed, if we are ever going to reach our full potential as a human race collectively. Our mere survival also depends on a paradigm shift because the path we're on currently is failing us badly. This isn't going to result in our favor. A lot of us already know this but are afraid to admit it. A paradigm shift occurs when a change of ideas, values, and disciplines take place. To change the quality of your life, a paradigm shift is necessary. Because continuing with the same blueprint will only result in more of what you have now.

To get something new, something different, something better... you have to change the framework. The whole process has to change from the foundation up. The blueprint must change first, in order to do that. Changing the paradigm is made possible by reprogramming the mind or through a process commonly known as "brainwashing." Now, let's take a closer look at brainwashing the mind. And it's not what you think. This is something we do to ourselves, as much as we allow others to do it to us, and we also do it to others.

Brainwashing is done using various techniques; in the next chapter we will look at the many ways we've been subverted by those we put into powerful positions with our support. Brace yourself, for what you are about to discover is very disturbing.

This next chapter will open your eyes and ears to what is going on behind the puppet show we refer to as "politics." For a long time, these stealth methods were kept quiet from the public (for obvious reasons). Now, politicians are *arrogantly* admitting their crimes against the citizens they swore to serve, with impunity... and they're doing it to your face, and on video! Yet somehow, we let these crimes continue and allow these criminals, disguised as law makers, to remain in power. How is this possible in a country founded on principals of civil rights and laws protecting liberty? *Shouldn't* people in those positions have any accountability? Especially, when they openly admit to their crimes?

"if you want to talk politics, we call it the "Wrapup Smear," You smear somebody... with falsehoods and... all the rest, and then you merchandise it." And then YOU write it, and they'll say: see, it was reported in the press... that this, this, this and this, so they have that validation, that the press reported the smear. And that is called the Wrap-up Smear."[44]

—Nancy Pelosi
(D-California, Minority Leader, 12th District – San Francisco)

In 2016, Ukrainian Prosecutor, **General Viktor Shokin**, in his investigation of corruption involving *Burisma Holdings*, a natural gas company, identified **Hunter Biden** as the recipient of over $3,000,000 from the company.[45] Joe Biden, during his presidential candidacy, was facing incriminating evidence of his dealings in foreign affairs, with his son, Hunter. At some point prior, Mr. Biden placed himself in front of cameras and proceeded to brag about an instance when he used US *"loan guarantees"* as *leverage* to remove a state prosecutor that was investigating crimes *involving his son in Ukraine*. Mr. Biden also goes on to say that he was successful in getting the Ukrainian government to install someone who would play along with them.

In a *thinking* society, this video evidence would *disqualify* Biden as a potential *presidential candidate*. It would also spark an independent and private investigation into the affairs of Mr. Biden all the way back to his first day in public office. Every criminal offense would be documented and Mr. Biden would enjoy the remainder of his life in a federal prison for his crimes. Sadly, he somehow won the election with the most votes ever recorded for a US president in history?[46] How is that possible?

---

44   "Pelosi admits to using "wrap up smear?" YouTube video, 0:52, posted byABC10News, October 10, 2018, accessed March 26, 2021, https://www.youtube.com/watch?v=W- zA-V_1lk40.
45   "Joe Biden Brags about getting Ukrainian Prosecutor Fired." YouTube video, 1:15, posted by dagalagas, September 20, 2019, accessed March 26, 2021, https://www.youtube.com/watch?v=UXA--dj2-CY.
46   Sophie Lewis, "Joe Biden breaks Obama's record for most votes ever cast for a U.S. presidential candidate," CBS News, December 7, 2020, accessed March 28, 2021, https://www. cbsnews.com/ news/joe-biden-popular-vote-record-barack-obama-us-presidential-election-donaldtrump

Former Vice President **Mike Pence** was asked by Journalist, **Tucker Carlson**, *"I know you're running for president. You are distressed the Ukrainians don't have enough American tanks. Every city in the United States has become much worse over the past three years. Drive around. There is not one city that has gotten better in the United States. And it's visible."* Tucker goes on to ask *"And yet you're concern is that the Ukrainians, a country that most people can't find on a map, who have received tens of billions of U.S. tax dollars, don't have enough tanks, I think it's fair to ask, where's the concern for the United States in that?"* To which Pence responded, *"Well, it's not my concern. Tucker I've heard that routine from you before, but it's not my concern. I'm running for President of the United States because I think this country is in a lot of trouble."*[47]

If the American people are not his concern, then what is this politician's purpose to serve the people he is not concerned about? And what kind of trouble will the country be in with *this guy* in charge? How do they continue to stay in power? Why aren't they being charged for their crimes? Why aren't they in prison? How else can this occur without mind manipulation?

It's an understatement to say that a paradigm shift is necessary... if humankind is to continue to exist.

47   Sean Moran, "Asked About Failing Cities by Tucker Carlson, Pence Says 'Not My Concern," Breitbart, July 14, 2023, accessed September 7, 2023, https://www.breitbart.com/politics/2023/07/14/mike-pence-says-crumbling-cities-not-my-concern-as-he-calls-for-more-aid-to-ukraine/

Chapter 11:
Brainwash Your Mind or Someone Else Will

Although hearing this sounds painful, you must know that it's happening to you now. Everything you watch, listen to, and read is being stored in your mind for later use. We are brainwashed from the moment of birth, all the way to taking our last breath. There is no way around it. Either you take control of what goes in or someone else will provide you with their own programs.

Watching TV is a favorite pastime for most of us. We do it for a way to unwind and relax... and we do it without a second thought. We watch crime shows, horror flicks, and other genres of violence for entertainment value. And though our conscious mind knows it's only scripted for our entertainment, our subconscious mind can't tell the difference between fantasy and reality. It takes in *everything*.

Feeding the mind is like feeding the body. One must be careful what goes in it. Not everything is healthy to feed on. The mind can easily be poisoned like the body. The mind feeds on ideas. So, if we apply positive ideas and cut out the negative messages from what we allow to enter, we feed our mind in a purposeful way. Until we are fully aware of how much control we have of what we allow in our minds, we will always be fed by situations and other people. If you think everything in your life is just fine and you don't need any improvements, look at the results.

Results Always Tell the Truth

Look at all areas of your life and ask yourself if you are really getting what you want. You can lie about it, or you can admit honestly that things could be *better*. **Results** will always tell the truth. The results are the scorecard of life. Just because the scores are low right now doesn't mean you are a loser. A low score only means that you need to *re-evaluate your process*. A win depends on how long you can stay in the game. But you must learn from your mistakes if you are to move past them. This can either be a setback, or a deeper hole to find your way out of.

Results are the steps toward success. If every step is a solid one, your success will last. If your process involves making sure every step is carefully scrutinized, you will see it in the results. One thing is certain... *results always tell the truth!* Every time you use the results to adjust your approach, you are another step closer to a victory.

The Exercise

You can do a Moral Character Inventory to expose self-defeating behavior patterns. But you must be brutally honest with yourself, *if you want to draw power from it*. These defects are identified in the form of shortcomings that are clearly visible once you analyze certain events and how you dealt with them. Trace the results and follow them back to their source cause, and you will outline areas where you fell short. Patterns that overlap or areas that repeat, are your *defects of character*. You can focus hard on those areas now that you know *exactly* what needs your attention. Or if you need help, **contact me**. Body building is a great example of visual results. There are those who want a hard body, and those who dream of having one. To sculpt a muscular body from a morbidly obese one is possible, but will require a great amount of work, commitment, and discipline. The "dreamer" will do all that is required in the beginning. After a week, he/ she will exhaust the level of motivation required to keep it going. The "doer" will set a schedule and keep it. After a week, the doer will experience the same moment of weakness, but will push himself/ herself through.

It's the process that makes the difference. Attitude also makes a difference in the results. Attitude is something that can't be compromised. If you are determined to achieve something, nothing will stand in your way. Your attitude towards the things you want in life will set the level of commitment for you to get it. But most of all... you *must* be aware of this golden nugget of knowledge, and be *willing* to apply it!

Success Blockers

Being in control of your mind is very important here. If you have outdated programs running in your subconscious, you want to *overwrite* them. Outdated programs are things we tell ourselves that don't apply anymore. Inconsistent thoughts create blockades in our path. When you tell yourself that you are a failure, or that you don't deserve success, that becomes a success blocker in your way. Success blockers are often found suppressed deep within the **subconscious mind**. Sometimes it's something we keep telling ourselves when we are feeling down. Most often it's someone else's opinion that we allowed our mind to snack on.

Finding the block might require hypnosis and/ or professional help. What I found helpful is the use of positive affirmations. This sounds silly, but positive affirmations do work. As long as your conscious mind believes it and doesn't reject it, the affirmation will be sent to the subconscious to be stored there. The more positive affirmations you have stored, the easier it is to purge the negative ones. Eventually, the negative messages will be overwritten and replaced by the positive ones.

Once the blocks are removed, the positive energy will flow freely. Happiness is the result of positive energy flow. I'm not saying you will never experience sadness or discomfort. You will know that those feelings will eventually pass, and how to flip the switch and find that happy place again. As you install new programs into the subconscious mind, you will find that your thinking patterns, behaviors, and reactions will change.

Set Your Mind for Success

Taking control of your own mind is the best gift you can give yourself. Nobody loves you more than you, and nobody knows what is really going on inside you better than you. Being controlled by other people, the media, society, or even religion isn't going to give you the life that you want or the health, wealth and happiness that you deserve. Your mind is the creation center. You just need to learn how to use it.

"You can do and have anything you set your mind to."

I hear people say that often. Most people will say that they agree with it. *Do you?* The truth behind this proverb is the programming of the mind. It's no secret. People have been using *mind control techniques* for centuries. The reason people haven't done more with their minds has a lot to do with the *distractions* that throw this capability out of focus.

There are so many distractions in any given day for every human being on the planet. Those of us that are tethered to social media through our phones, tablets, and computers, will have the hardest time placing our focus on the *inside world*. As technology evolves, the human element seems to be choked out of the process. Our distain for human life really shows through, and this should disturb you. If you look objectively into the past, you will find patterns of thought and behavior that have led humans down a very dark path. Let's examine this closer together... *shall we?*

Dangerous Ideology

Today, we see hatred and violence in all flavors. Hate groups are granted special permits to gather *peacefully* to spew their poison onto society. It is their right under the freedom of speech in this country. **Free speech** is necessary and must be protected to ensure a free society. But, when it's used to spread hatred and bigotry, it should awaken society to the motives of those who use it in that manner.

In 1865, a group of confederate veterans formed a secret society that quickly grew to become the domestic terrorist organization known as the Ku Klux Klan. The KKK is responsible for intimidation, destruction of property, assault, and murder. Their targets were African Americans and white republicans. The KKK engaged in terrorist raids at night, bent on reversing the federal government's policies to grant rights to the local African American population.

The KKK resurfaced again during the increased immigration in the 1910s and 1920s. They also displayed their hatred and violence during the Civil Rights Movement in the 1950s and 1960s.[48] This hate group is still alive and well today, and it continues to recruit and brainwash the

---

48   History. Com Staff, "KKK Founded," History.com, A+E Networks, 2010, accessed August 23,2017, http://www.history.com/this-day-in-history/kkk-founded.

minds of anyone that fits their model. They even go as far as starting their training and conditioning with children old enough to walk.

History Lesson: Indoctrination of Radical Ideology

Adolf Hitler joined the German Workers' Party in 1919. He was thirty years of age and determined to make it succeed. In October of 1919, Hitler had just over a hundred people to show up at a German Workers' Party meeting held in a beer cellar. By the end of 1920 the name of the group was changed to the Nazi Party with over three thousand members.[49] Hitler knew how to speak to a crowd. He was also well versed in the art of manipulation. He would wait for crowds to quiet down, and then shout amid the silence. He would repeat messages over and over again to press on his points.[50] The Nazis used propaganda and made sure the Jews were made to appear as parasites. Hitler eventually convinced Germany and the rest of the world that *exterminating* an entire race of people from the planet was a *good idea.*

Of course, that idea didn't sit well for very long, especially in the west. He was eventually forced to stop his killing spree by the Soviet army and the Americans. Although America was involved in putting an end to the Nazis in Germany and throughout Europe, it has made a comfortable home for them here in the United States.

The American Nazi Party is alive and well right here at home. As much as we would like to believe that Americans loathe the Nazis and their cause, the facts point toward something much different. Hate groups like the KKK and the Nazis are only a part of a much larger problem in our country. There are nearly a thousand hate groups in America according to the reports from the Southern Poverty Law Center.[51]

---

49   Philip Gavin, "The Rise of Adolf Hitler," The History Place,1996, accessed August 23, 2017, http://www.historyplace.com/worldwar2/riseofhitler/party.htm.
50   Pema Dechen Rapten, "The Rise of the Nazi Party,1933," Mount Holyoke College, access August 23, 2017, https://www.mtholyoke.edu/~rapte22p/classweb/interwarperiod/nazi- party.html.
51   Ryan Struyk, "By the numbers: 7 charts that explain hate groups in the United States," CNN, last modified August 15, 2017, access August 23, 2017, http://www.cnn. com/2017/08/14/politics/charts-explain-us-hate-groups/index.html.

Hatred: Poison to the Mind and Cancer to Society

It's very clear that we are easily manipulated to believe the most ridiculous nonsense. This is only possible because we let the ideas of others take over our minds. Hatred is not a natural emotion. We are creatures of love energy. We all want to be loved and to love. Hatred is a learned response, and a ***dangerous*** one.

Today, hate groups pop up as people find more things to hate. Hatred has gotten out of control. The acts of violence make it worse. If the results of all this bitterness and anger aren't enough to wake us, what more will it take? Are we going to continue to destroy each other? *Is this the best we can do with our minds?*

The result of a poisoned mind is cancer to a society. Also, every mind that becomes poisoned feeds that cancer. We experience the physical effects of poisoned minds every day. We can sense the anger building inside when we watch a video of someone being hurt. We can feel our blood pressure go up as we witness another act of violence or a crime take place. By now, I hope you can see just how bad things get when we feed the frenzy without thinking of the aftermath. We all have the ability to re-program our own mind and shift our paradigm to a better way to think and live. *What is taking us so long to do it?*

Why after seeing so much death and destruction, suffering, pain, and despair, do we *do nothing*? Why do we fuel the propaganda with our own misinformation and ignorance? Why do we help spread that propaganda on social media? Is pressing forward an agenda of social cancer and civil unrest our greatest idea? Or are we under the influence of something more **sinister**?

A Toxic Relationship Involving Mind Control Agendas

The forces that work within governments have displayed the lack of value to human life on more than *hundreds* of occasions. For people to believe that their own government would never do anything to harm them is *more* than naïve. Throughout history, governments around the world have made it very clear, that its agenda isn't always in their people's best interest. Even our own government has displayed this behavior pattern over the decades. Too many events have unfolded in the public eye to ignore the signs of *this* truth. And though *evidence* of **cover-up** remains present, *people still side and support those who inflict the most harm to them, and all of us!* Many people who have openly criticized these signs of foul play have been labeled as conspiracy nuts and are mocked or laughed at. The term "*Conspiracy Theory.*" refers to any other possible explanation other than the **official** one. Even if the alternate theory makes more sense, it's still a conspiracy theory, unless *the authorities* say it's not. And those authorities don't include doctors, scientists, military or law enforcement personnel, building engineers, demolition experts, or anyone else that isn't a high-ranking government official. See how silly that sounds? In a free country, aren't **We the People** *supposed* to be the authority? How did we become so lost?

The social engineers know their job and do it well. We have been bombarded with *psychological warfare* attacks since many of us have been alive! Unbeknownst to us, these ridiculous policies have been enforced as a result of our silence and loyal obedience. Nobody has ever thought to question the morality or the legality of even the most bizarre policy presented. Once the bill is signed into law, then it is what it is. REALLY??? If you don't see why we are where we are, keep reading.

Pro-Government; Anti-Oligarchy

Government, only has administrative duties. A system of government in a free nation does not rule its people. That would be like your boss answering to his/her employees. That's not how it works. In America, there are laws that govern our government. When government steps outside of its boundaries and begins to violate the rights of the people, it is committing a crime. Everyone involved in that crime must be removed and punished immediately.

When a criminal commits murder, he does not get a *pay raise or a bonus*. He is **charged and punished**. People in powerful positions must be held liable for their crimes too. *However, the punishment should be much* *stiffer*, because **abuse of power** should carry a *much harsher* sentence. It should be this way in order to keep government power *in check* by the people. Currently, government votes on everything, and the people don't get a voice in any of the matters effecting their daily lives. All of this goes on while the voiceless people are being taxed out of their homes and on to the street.

Criminals have been in control for a long time, and now they are using any means necessary to stay in control. After the events that took place in 2020, we can clearly see that *voting* for government officials is pointless. Governments do not rule their constituents. Dictators do... and when multiple dictators are in power, we call them "oligarchs." Oligarchs believe they can rule over others as they please. When you begin to understand the terms used and what they mean, the big picture comes into focus. And then you will realize the *magnitude* of the hole we are in!

The world is in the grip of a **totalitarian oligarchy**. This isn't news. It's been this way for a long while. When you hear the term "*tyranny*," this is referring to life under totalitarian rule. Oligarchs are the warlords that keep everyone in line, because there is no freedom. So many people don't believe the United States will ever fall from its pedestal as a world superpower. It saddens me to inform you...that *America has already fallen*. In 2020, the citizens of the **United States of America** experienced events that should never take place in a *free* society.

The use of emergency powers suddenly opened a doorway for violation after *obscene* violation by local governments against its own citizens. You would think, if we had a system governed by laws that keep government powers in check, this would *never* happen.

What was most shocking was the blind obedience by the masses of the mindless. Blind obedience and willful ignorance will send a free nation spinning into the abyss of tyranny on a scale the world hasn't seen yet. It's been a few centuries since the US has seen such brutality on its own soil. The British oligarchs didn't leave without a fight. And not too long ago 6 million people were systematically murdered while the world sat silent and did nothing! Maybe we need this as a wake-up-call? How are things like this possible in a *civil* society?

Keep reading... this chapter will open your eyes and blow your mind wide open! These are some of the *darkest* secrets exposed in open daylight for you. You may want to digest it *slowly*.

America's Founding Fathers

The brave men who put their lives on the line when they put their names in ink, granted every citizen the right to life and liberty. Back then, the brutality of government tyranny was *fresh* on everyone's mind. They created a system of law that *limits* the **power of government** *and gives the power to the people* it serves. This concept of a **constitutional republic** became revered across every nation in the world, and their people... *except* the king of England.

Today, there are groups that rally to take away those rights. Their belief is that government knows best, and they should provide and control everything for the people. This idea of government having absolute control, not only undermines everything the founding fathers stood and fought for, it also ignores every time when absolute power in government led to tyranny in the past. Are we that blind... or just *stupid*? 2020 was a test to see how far society can be *pushed towards* that dangerous idea. Ironically, the rhetoric used to market this to an unsuspecting public was "to save lives" when all it did was destroy lives. *Is this normal*? Because this was said to become the "new normal."

History can teach us so much of where we are and where we want to be. By studying history, we can see what worked and what *didn't*. This invaluable tool should be sought after and respected. Instead, it's mocked, denied and in some cases erased. In a society where freedom is revered, how would this seem *acceptable*?

Erasing History

In the last few years, we have seen monuments taken down across the country. Confederate flags are now considered to be symbols of racism.

Some people are even offended by the American flag. It seems like people are in support of erasing history that is offensive. Some sources even deny events that took place. Unfortunately, removing statues, flags, or burning books will not erase the acts of injustice. In fact, removing these monuments and written documents from our past only puts the lessons we need to learn farther away from our minds. Now who would want to do such a thing?

The only logic that fits the idea of erasing history is sinister. We can learn from the harsh and brutal lessons of the past, as offensive as they are. Erasing history is how history repeats. The science behind it is self-explanatory. Those who push for censorship have a hidden agenda. What they're doing goes beyond hiding truth by erasing history. All anyone has to do to learn more about history is to dig. Unfortunately, powerful forces are keeping people in the darkness with surprisingly little resistance. How is this possible? You are *limited* with the data you are *spoon fed*. If you want facts, you need to become a detective yourself!

The lessons we can learn from history will establish the documented capabilities of man. If left unchecked, we all become victim to our own devices. Critical thinking also comes from the same lessons. If we cripple ourselves in ways of critical thought, then we are surely at the end of the line. Because critical thinkers are less likely to become *human livestock*.

Forgotten History

It was not that long ago when a group of radical supremacists took over Germany, and then most of western Europe, then marched into Russia. These psychopaths systemically murdered more than 6 million or more people they labeled as "Jews."

Death camps were set up all over Germany and Poland, as tens of thousands of people were transported into the camps by railroad. After being labeled and placed in ghettos, the passengers left their ghetto homes with most of their valuables. They were greeted by Nazi soldiers and told to take a shower. Unbeknownst to them, the showers were *gas chambers* that were designed to look like showers. What evil brilliance went into that kind of thought? The idea of mass murdering people by trickery came from the thoughts of only a few men. But it took the rest of the world to allow it to happen... and continue to go on.

"Selection" of Hungarian Jews on the ramp at Auschwitz-II (Birkenau), Poland during the German occupation, May/June 1944. Jews were sent either to work or to the gas chamber. The photograph is part of the collection known as the Auschwitz Album. See Auschwitz Album, Yad Vashem: "The Auschwitz Album is the only surviving visual evidence of the process leading to mass murder at Auschwitz-Birkenau."

The collection as a whole was first published as The Auschwitz Album in 1980 in the United States, Canada and elsewhere, by the Nazi hunter Serge Klarsfeld, but individual images had been published before that – for example, during the 1947 Auschwitz trial in Poland and the 1963–1965 Frankfurt Auschwitz trials. It is not known when this particular image was first published.

Date: May or June 1944, Auschwitz-Birkenau, Poland

Source: Yad Vashem. The album was donated to Yad Vashem by Lili Jacob (later Lili Jacob-Zelmanovic Meier, a survivor, who found it in the Mittelbau-Dora concentration camp in 1945.

Author: Unknown. Several sources believe the photographer to have been Ernst Hoffmann or Bernhard Walter of the SS

Camp in Birkenau, Poland during the German occupation, a group of Jews walking towards the gas chambers and crematoria 2 and 3, 27/05/1944. Photographs documenting the arrival process of Hungarian Jews from the Tet Ghetto in Auschwitz-Birkenau extermination camp.

Date: 27 May 1944

Source: Auschwitz Album ([https://collections.ushmm.org/search/catalog/pa8538 record in USHMM collection).

Author: anonymous, possibly SS photographers E. Hoffmann & B. Walter.

Today, we see powerful money-rich people monopolizing on basic need items such as food, water, and medicine. Some are very open about their belief in eugenics and transhumanism. It does not take *common-core algebra* to figure out what is happening. As we die by their hand, they get more money-rich. And until we learn the forgotten lessons from our history... it will continue to repeat.

Food for Thought

Absolute government power over every aspect of society isn't freedom at all. In fact, the more that government provides everything *they* feel you need, the more control they have over your life and the way you live. Study history and you will see how freedom turned to tyranny in other societies. If you think it could never happen *here*, ask yourself how did it happen **there**?

Are you offended easily by statues, history, or the truth? It's time you begin to shed that thin-skinned mentality. There are events that have taken place that are very offensive to the senses. But, like a strong cup of coffee... it will awaken you! Instead of being offended into denial, use these tragic events to access your sixth sense... ***intuition***. Critical thinking happens only when you rely mostly on things you know without a doubt. Here are some things we can all agree on:

- Evil does exist, but not everyone is evil.
- We have all experienced crime to some degree.
- Criminals choose personal gain over the rights of anyone else or any rule of law.

Here is where we expand our thinking...

- Criminals can also succeed in business and politics, and can be elected as our leaders.
- If a criminal became a law maker, imagine the damage that could result from that.
- Criminals in control of banking and world markets make the rules because they control the money. They can also manipulate markets, and other people in power because of this.
- Criminals in powerful positions can hire low-level criminals to do their dirty-work.
- Not all criminals are purely evil. Some are just desperate, and desperation drives people to do bad things.

- Criminals work inside of our government. Some are evil, most are only desperate.

If you still can't bring yourself to accept that government wouldn't do anything to harm its own people, then look up these moments in history that are conveniently covered up and hidden from the public. Apply critical thinking and add it all up. Not everything you were told was true. Most of it was made up to keep you quiet and calm. If everyone knew the extent of the damage, the devils on the surface would all be sent back to hell! Below are examples of government in violation of its limits.

History Lesson: Alcohol Prohibition

During the Alcohol Prohibition, the government became frustrated with the number of people consuming alcohol. Even after the manufacture, sale, and transportation of alcohol was banned, the number of alcohol consumers soared higher than before its prohibition. As a scare tactic to get people to stop drinking, the American government began to poison certain alcohol. The contaminated supplies resulted in the death of over ten thousand of its own citizens.[52] That's just one instance of malice. Here are a few more examples of government power over the mind of its people.

History Lesson: Marijuana Prohibition

The idea of prohibition in a free society seems awkward just by itself. But when a government wants to prohibit its citizens from using anything that has more benefits to the quality of life than side effects, the people should question the motive. Research has shown that the cannabis plant has healing properties. The U.S. Drug Enforcement Administration's fact sheet on the drug says that "No death from overdose of marijuana has been reported." So why did they classify it as a Schedule I drug along with

---

52   Daven Hiskey, "The American Government Once Intentionally Poisoned Certain Alcohol Supplies Resulting in the Death of Over 10,000 American Citizens," Today I Found Out, July 30, 2010, accessed August 27, 2017, http://www.todayifoundout.com/index.php/2010/07/the-american-government-once-intentionally-poisoned-certain-alcohol-supplies-resulting-in-the-death-of-over-10000-american-citizens/.

Heroin, Meth, and LSD?[53] This led to the Marijuana Tax Act of 1937, which effectively banned its use and sales.[54]

Reefer Madness

Reefer Madness started out as a film to be shown to parents teaching them about the dangers of cannabis use. The original film was called "Tell Your Children, "and it was financed by a church group as a morality tale. In 1936 it was released as a *propaganda* film revolving around events that take place when high school students are lured by pushers to try marijuana. In the film, after smoking one marijuana cigarette, the lead character is hooked. His new addiction leads him down a path to self- destruction. The film suggests marijuana use leads to crimes and other things like hit and run car accidents, manslaughter, suicide, teen sex, attempted rape, hallucinations, and an overall descent into madness due to marijuana addiction.

Duck and Cover

Duck and Cover was taught to the American people in response to growing concerns regarding global thermonuclear war. Duck and Cover drills continued throughout the 1960s. Eventually, people were told to build bomb shelters. If you didn't have one, you got a four-day supply of food, water and first-aid and were told to stay indoors and away from windows. This advice was known to be inadequate, but the Civil Defense Administration continued to encourage it anyway.[55] Can you imagine the number of casualties following this advice, if there were actual nuclear strikes in populated areas? Why aren't we learning from our past?

53   "Drug Scheduling," United States Drug Enforcement Administration, accessed May 10, 2018, https://www.dea.gov/druginfo/ds.shtml
54   DR. Malik Burnett and Amanda Reiman, PHD, MSW, "How Did Marijuana Become Illegal in the First Place?" Drug Policy Alliance, October 8, 2014, accessed May 10, 2018, http://www.drugpolicy.org/blog/how-did-marijuana-become-illegal-first-place.
55   Kate Kelly, "Remember Duck and Cover? What Safety Experts May Have Been Thinking," Huffington Post, last modified May 25, 2011, accessed August 21, 2017, http://www. huffingtonpost.com/kate-kelly/remember-duck-and-cover-w_b_774134.html.

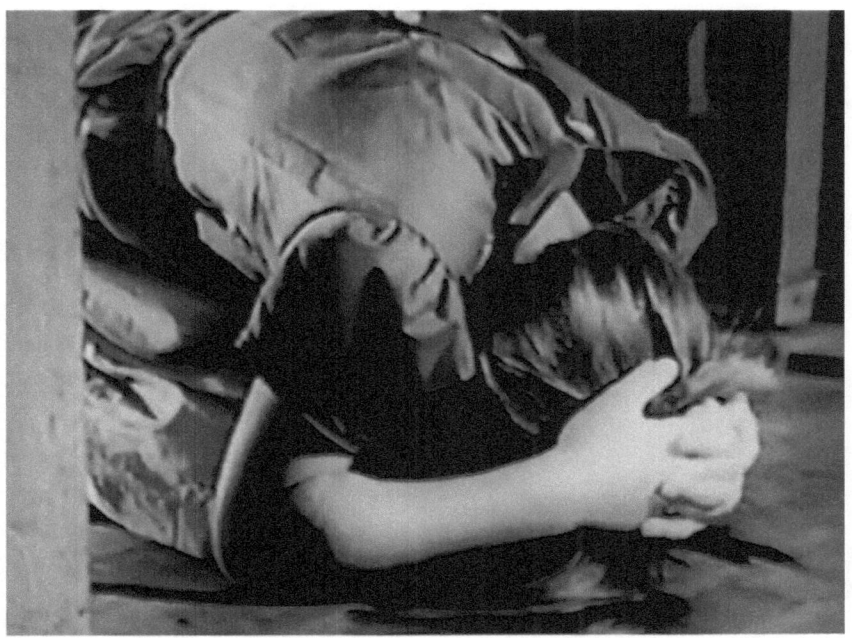

Mask Mandates Following a Plan-demic

In 2020, the citizens of the United States of America, and the rest of the world, blindly believed the words of their government officials. Even after witnessing inconsistencies, and in some cases... documented crimes. Many were fooled into thinking the misinformation being pumped out as propaganda was *science*.

The mask debate is as *dumb* as the gun debate, but some people cannot see that. Debating the facts we know against politics is foolish and *dangerous*. There should be no debate. Facts are *facts*. Science involves an open mind and brutal honesty. Universal laws govern science. For us to fully understand science we need to tune *inward* toward our most trusted tool, *instinct*. We are not taught how to do that, and to make matters more difficult, we are kept distracted in all directions to keep us from ever seeing the light of truth. Brutal honesty requires a lot of courage. But then, once we become honest with ourselves, then our loyalty must shift to doing what we know is right. And that is what keeps most of us stuck.

We are gambling away any chance of a future for our own children, and their children! We better learn the science... or we will bury their dreams with ours! Blind obedience to these harmful measures will seal our fate.

Pay Attention to What's Happening

The three types of masks recommended for the prevention of spreading the coronavirus (according to local mandates and media), are the paper surgical mask, the N95, and the cloth. Prior to 2020, the United States Department of Labor, Occupational Safety & Health Administration (OSHA), used to regulate all businesses for safety and health related issues...including the *usage of respiratory devices* such as those mentioned above and more. Oxygen deficient atmospheres used to matter back then, but not so much now? Companies were being fined huge sums for the usage of the wrong kind of mask for the work environment.

Lawsuits associated with digital ADA (Americans with Disabilities Act) compliance are on the rise. More than 4000 ADA *website* lawsuits listed by the end of 2023![56] This involves website accessibility to the sight and hearing impaired. However, there are literally tens of millions of people with breathing disabilities such as Asthma, and other respiratory diseases. How do universal mask mandates measure up to *those disabilities*? Breathing is a higher level of priority, or *should* be. Also, if credibility matters, then there must be a **universal mission**, not a universal mandate that forces people with breathing disabilities to restrict their breathing. This *double standard* has tarnished the reputation of the ADA, and every other organization that compromises their integrity to their mission. People do not get to choose their disabilities. There is no *medical* reason to force people to cover their face. Our science and medical community should already know this, given their level of education, training, and on the job experience.

---

56   Gus Alexiou, "Website Accessibility Lawsuits Rising Exponentially In 2023 According To Latest Data," Forbes, last modified Jun 30, 2023, accessed Sept 5, 2023, https://www.forbes.com/sites/gusalexiou/2023/06/30/website-accessibility-lawsuits-rising-exponentially-in-2023-according-to-latest-data/?sh=441b88057117f.

Facts We Know

Surgical masks are *useless* outside of a **sterile** environment. I know doctors wear them, but they do not wear them outside of the operating room… at least they never used to prior to 2020. The conditions are very different inside of a sterile room, in a restricted area, inside of a medical facility, then the one at your local Walmart.

The N95 mask is designed for contaminated areas. If you have an illness you want to keep from others, this one will let you blow it through a check-valve in the side of the mask. So, there's that. The N95 will filter out 95% of contaminates, but you will feel the effects from lack of oxygen after several minutes. Long term use can result in hypoxia and other harmful conditions related to a lack of oxygen saturation in the blood. This condition is *extremely* harmful to your heart, brain, and liver. If the hypoxia is severe, irreversible damage can begin within 4 hours.[57] Hypoxia is also known to affect your body's *natural* immune system.[58] And you need that to fight off a virus!

57　Lynne Eldrige, MD," Overview and Types of Hypoxia," Very well Health, last modified October 22, 2022, accessed April 6, 2021, https://www.verywellhealth.com/hypox-ia-types-symptoms-and-causes-2248929.

58　Cormac T. Taylor, Sean P. Colgan, "Regulation of immunity and inflammation by hypoxia in immunological niches," Nature Reviews Immunology, published October 3, 2017, accessed April 6, 2021, https://www.nature.com/articles/nri.2017.103?foxtrotcall- back=true#citeas.

The human body inhales oxygen and exhales carbon dioxide. Masking for long periods will have an effect on this natural process of maintaining life we call "breathing." Reputable medical professionals have come out and risked their licenses and careers to get the truth out to the public that began to embrace the idea as a fashion accessory.

The cloth masks are the ***most hazardous***, as they collect harmful bacteria and bodily waste and offer 0% protection from even your own germs. Yet, this one seems to be the most popular because of the individuality offered in the many colors and designs. Interesting concept: Designer killing cloths? The people love them! Do you see the programming yet? If so, then why are we allowing these psychopaths to lay harm to us and *force* us to harm our own children?

Photo taken by Leo Fontes.

Conspiracy *Theory* or Conspiracy?

If you or someone you know use the term "conspiracy theory," it's time to break it down to its definition and context.

con·spir·a·cy
/kənˈspirəsē/
Noun
1. a secret plan by a group to do something unlawful or harmful.

the·o·ry
/ˈTHirē/
Noun
1. a plausible or scientifically acceptable general principle or body of principles offered to explain phenomena.

The term **conspiracy theory** is used to thwart off questioning around every suspicious event since the JFK assassination. Some believe it was in this timeline when the term was first coined. It would make sense as to why those working in the shadows would want less attention to the sketchy details of their stealth operations... especially when the punishment for the crime could involve **execution**. When the stakes are *that* high, all options stay on the table... even mass murder... or at least to *silence* those who know, or learn *too much*.

Evidence changes theory to fact. As evidence piles up, the theory begins to look more like a conspiracy. The term conspiracy theorist is nothing more than a fancy word for private investigator. The only threat an investigator can impose are to those committing crimes. If we can all agree that corruption is everywhere, and that criminals exist in all areas of life and all levels of powerful positions, then why are we so quick to dismiss every questionable or obvious criminal act? It would make sense that unless you are involved in the crimes taking place against the American people, you should be questioning those committing crimes, not those asking the logical questions.

False Flag Operations
Some believe that the events that took place in 2020 just prior to a US presidential election was a false flag operation. False flags are commonly used for tricking people into supporting a fictitious story to justify a world changing event. In most cases these staged events do result in actual casualties. But, with the rise of technology, there are private firms now that offer services to stage a safer option. I found this website interesting: **https://crisiscast.com/solutions/** I'm not implying this

particular company is involved in wrongdoings, but the technology is definitely available to make it *possible*. I do understand that there is a need to make training videos for emergency staff.[59] But, knowing this takes me back to a question of ethics and integrity... which seems to be rare these days.

False flags are real and have been used in the past. You may be saying: *this is complete bullshit!* I don't blame you for thinking that. I'm sure you've heard "the truth is often stranger than fiction. There is a lot of truth to that statement. Although we may never know the whole truth, events that were thought to be terrorist attacks perpetrated by an outside enemy are coming into light as being an "inside job." It is hard to accept that our own government would betray the people in partaking in such heinous crimes such as mass murder and genocide. But history will prove that is not a far reach to think so.

A False Flag Operation is a staged attack, usually by a government acting as a targeted enemy, against its own people. These covert operations are designed to deceive the public in such a way that it appears that the attacks are genuinely made by the false enemy. False Flag Operations have been used many times throughout history. It's usually used as a justification to go to war.[60] However, this type of operation has been used for other purposes.

Hitler used **Operation Himmler**, as a *false flag* to justify the invasion of Poland. Also, on February 27, 1933, the **Reichstag fire**, which was an arson fire falsely blamed as a "Communist effort to overthrow the state," justified Hitler's seizure of power and suspension of liberties.[61]

> *"The only one who really knows about the Reichstag is I, because I set it on fire!"*[62]

—Hermann Goring

---

59 EMS1 Staff, "What are crisis actors?" EMS1, May 4, 2018, accessed April 5, 2021, https://www.ems1.com/mass-casualty-incidents-mci/articles/what-are-crisis-actors9DwQ3kdMYgUo66w.

60 WantToKnow.info Staff, "False Flag: Summary of False Flag Operations and False Flag Terrorism," WantToKnow.info, accessed August 24, 2017, http://www.wanttoknow.info/falseflag.

61 United States Holocaust Memorial Museum, "The Reichstag Fire," Holocaust Encyclopedia, accessed August 24, 2017, https://www.ushmm.org/wlc/en/article.php?Modu-IeId=1000765.

62 "Hermann Goring Quotes and Sayings - Page 1," Inspiring Quotes, accessed March 29, 2021, https://www.inspiringquotes.us/author/6917-hermann-goring.

The Bali attack in 2002 is said to be a False Flag Operation. Former Indonesian president, Abdurrahman Wahid, admitted in an interview with SBS's Dateline program, about links between Indonesian authorities and terrorist groups.[63]

A 2005 bookstore explosion in southeastern Turkey is believed to be a False Flag Operation, blaming a rebel group to justify a crackdown on that group. When the citizens pieced together what really took place, the attack sparked days of rioting that left four more people dead.[64]

In July of 1954, an Israeli terrorist cell operating in Egypt, launched a campaign to bomb several buildings including American diplomatic facilities. The thugs left behind evidence pointing to the Arabs as the perpetrators. When one of the bombs went off by accident, the Egyptians were able to identify the real suspects which led to the shakedown of Israel's Defense Minister along with the entire Israeli government.[65]

If you think this kind of deception could never happen here in the US, you need to wake up and start drinking pots of coffee until you can't fall back asleep! Some sources have ruled the events that took place in America on **September 11, 2001** was a false flag operation.[66] New evidence has shown that the official story cannot hold against the laws of science and logic.[67] It certainly helped our government go to war with an invisible enemy, and to strip away our *right to privacy*.

False Flag Operations occur everywhere around the world, including the US. The use of fear to motivate people and to steer them like livestock is nothing new. Mind control is a reality. False Flag Operations have been used for centuries because they work. Also, because most people prefer

---

63   Sydney Morning Herald, "Possible police role in 2002 Bali attack," October 12, 2005, accessed August 24, 2017, https://www.smh.com.au/national/possible-police-role-in-2002-bali-attack-20051013-gdm8qg.html

64   Turkish Daily News, "Court says senior officers involved in Semdinli bombing," last modified January 5 2008, accessed August 24, 2017, https://www.wanttoknow.info/documents/false_flag_turkey.

65   Jewish Virtual Library, "Israel Military Intelligence: The Lavon Affair (Summer 1954)," accessed August 24, 2017, http://www.jewishvirtuallibrary.org/the-lavon-affair.

66   Douglas Yates, "9/11 was a false-flag event; war was the hidden agenda," Daily News Miner, last modified September 12, 2017, accessed May 8, 2018, https://www.newsminer.com/opinion/community_perspectives/9-11-was-a-false-flag-event-war-was-the-hidden-agenda/article_13f614aa-9789-11e7-8277-7b0b994cb144.html

67   Dr. Graeme MacQueen, "118Witnesses: The Firefighters' Testimony to Explosions in the Twin Towers," 2500+ Architects & Engineers for 9/11 Truth, last modified August 21, 2006, accessed May 8, 2018, https://ic911.org/journal/articles/118-witnesses-the-firefighters-testimony-to-explosions-in-the-twin-towers/

to remain in the dark rather than to do the work to stay informed. There isn't a need to change something that has worked so well, for so long, and on so many! Looking back, *we should have known better...*

Although false flags go well beyond the threshold of despicable, there are those who push the limits of terrorism to new lows. **Psychological warfare** has been used since early man in the form of *fear*. The sheer brutality and barbarianism of our early rulers came from very dark places. Killing in cold blood seemed to be a good way to keep people in line. With the advancement of technology came stealth methods of mass killing. Also, the ability to control the human mind became an obsession for the psychopaths that rule behind the curtain. *If you can control the minds of the many, they become your slaves willingly. If you can control even one mind, you can manipulate many more with just one event.* This is how they think.

Project MK-Ultra

The origins of this program are traced back to *Monarch Programming*, which is a combination of psychology, neuroscience, and occult rituals to create an alter persona within a victim, that can be triggered and controlled by handlers. One of the first systematic studies on trauma-based mind control were directed by **Josef Mengele**, *a Nazi physician* that was responsible for performing grisly human experiments on camp inmates during the Holocaust. Mengele's work would become the foundation for a new program called Project MK-Ultra.[68]

Project MK-Ultra was a top-secret government project conducted by the CIA in which hundreds of experiments were done on American citizens, some of which were illegal. In 1953, Allan Dulles, director of the Central Intelligence Agency, approved Project MK-Ultra.[69] The program involved psychedelic drugs, paralytics, and electroshock therapy. Sometimes the test subjects knew about their participation, but most often they did not. This was said to have gone on between 1953 to 1964

---

68   Kevin Canfield, "The Sinister Scientist Behind the CIA's Mind-Control Mayhem," Daily Beast, last modified November 30, 2019, accessed September 5, 2023, https://www.thedailybeast.com/the-sinister-scientist-behind-the-cias-mind-control-mayhem.
69   Kim Zetter, "April 13, 1953: CIA OKs MK-ULTRA Mind-Control Tests," Wired, April 13 2010, accessed August 21, 2017, https://www.wired.com/2010/04/0413mk-ultra-authorized/

and officially shut down in 1973, but other reports show activity well into the late 1980's and into the 1990's. Due to poor record keeping and *destroyed documents*, we will never really know just *how many* people were victimized by our government.[70]

Manchurian Candidates

Manchurian Candidates are highly conditioned, trained, and dangerous MK-Ultra sleeper assassins. In some cases, they are used as a patsy or a scapegoat for high profile assassinations or mass shooting events. A mind controlling facility was set up in Australia as a school for children. It was founded and directed by **Anne Hamilton-Byrne** and known as *The Family*. When Australian Federal police raided the school in 1987, they found more than a dozen children that were brought up in complete isolation. The kids were all half-starved, beaten and forced to take tranquilizers and LSD.[71]

The use of torture removes the memory of the training and the objective. Through the process of disassociation, the dominant part of your personality goes to sleep, as a *defense mechanism*. This is a normal human response to trauma.[72] Programmed sleepers aren't aware that they are agents and live a normal life until triggered by a programmed sound or command.

One child that was known to be raised in *The Family* by *Hamilton-Byrne* is **Julian Assange**.[73] The man behind **WikiLeaks** is a programmer turned hacker, that was accessing government networks and bank mainframes. He was arrested in 1991 after being charged with more than 30 criminal counts related to his hacking. Facing 10 years in prison,

70   6 MelissaBlevins, "Project Mk ultra: One of the Most Shocking CIA Programs of All Time," Gizmodo, September 23, 2013, accessed August 21, 2017, https://gizmodo.com/project-mkultra-one-of-the-most-shocking-cia-programs-1370236359.

71   7 Sebastain Edward, "MK-Ultra Project, Monarch and Julian Assange," Medium, January 19, 2015, accessed May 11, 2018, https://medium.com/@sebastianedward/mk-ultra-project-monarch-and-julian-assange-ad2aa42ba1a4. ALSO https://steemit.com/mk-ultra/@alive125/mk-ultra-project-monarch-and-julian-assange.

72   "MK ULTRA Sleeper Assassin Confession: Government Scopolamine Secrets," You Tube video, 54:27, posted by "The Lip TV," August 30, 2015, https://www.youtube.com/watch?v=Sau-pl_OI3o.

73   Spike1138, "Who Exactly is "JulianAssange"..?"NewsSpike,June29,2013,AccessedMay 14, 2018, http://spikethenews.blogspot.com/2013/06/who-exactly-is-assange.html

Assange struck a plea deal.[74] Over the years, Assange has been in and out of trouble for exposing secrets and annoying those trying to hide them.

Another possible resident under the control of **Anne Hamilton-Byrne** and *The Family* was **Martin Bryant**, the *alleged* Port Arthur massacre shooter. Bryant, who pled guilty to murdering 35 people and injuring 21 others, was an intellectually impaired young man with an IQ of 66. In addition to that, the Tasmanian Police Service still does not have a single legally valid eyewitness identification, to this day.[75]

Coincidentally, it just so happened to be the Port Arthur shooting event that led to Australia's new gun control policy. Like the US, Australia also had a high rate of private gun ownership. After a mass shooting event in Dublane, Scotland, and the shooting event in Port Arthur just weeks later, the ruling center-right Liberal Party joined with groups from across the political spectrum to work on legislation that would make owning guns more difficult.[76]

There isn't much information easily available that ties Martin Bryant to The Family, or Hamilton-Byrne, other than a few articles using the same information. This could be because sources were either silenced, or the information was carefully removed. A lot of things changed in Australia as a result of this high-profile event. Information getting out could be damaging for those intending to disarm the citizens of the free world. We saw what took place in Australia in 2020. Maybe the set up for a hostile tyrannical take-over involves a few steps over a long period of time? Why so long? People forget easily.

Sleeper Assassins or Just Pawns in a Bigger Game?

MK Ultra victim from Toronto, Canada named **Matthew Pauly**, describes his experience on *Coast-to-Coast AM* with **George Noory**. During this interview, his connection is abruptly cut off and the show producers tried

74   Scott Bland, "Julian Assange: the hacker who created WikiLeaks, "The Christian Science Monitor, July 26, 2010, accessed May 14, 2018, https://www.csmonitor.com/USA/Military/2010/0726/Julian-Assange-the-hacker-who-created-WikiLeaks

75   Carl Wernerhoff, "Was Martin Bryant Framed?", The Port Arthur Massacre, Nexus Magazine, Volume 13, Number 4, last modified July 2006, accessed September 5, 2023, http://www.whale.to/b/wernerhoff.html

76   Krishnadev Calamur, "Australia's Lessons on Gun Control," The Atlantic, October 2, 2017, accessed May 14, 2018, https://www.theatlantic.com/international/archive/2017/10/australia-gun-control/541710/

to get him on his landline, cell phone and even Skype...the entire internet connection had gone out right. George thought the guy had been shot![77]

Some people believe that **Lee Harvey Oswald**, the alleged assassin that killed President Kennedy, was indeed a Manchurian Candidate. Oswald claimed his innocence, but before he ever made it to trial, he was gunned down by another assassin named Jack Ruby (who was also shot to death before he could be questioned). Today, after thousands of hours of investigation and research of the evidence surrounding the murder of President John F. Kennedy, the Lone Gunman Theory has been ruled out as fiction. All of Oswald's behaviors reflected the *characteristics* of a Manchurian Candidate.[78]

Some people claim to have found implants *mysteriously* planted in their bodies. Dr. Rauni Kilde, Former Chief Medical Officer in Finland, has seen such devices and believes people are used in covert mind control experiments. She goes on to say that implants today are much smaller and easier to plant. Also, placing them in the backs of people makes them much harder to detect because they won't show on autopsies.[79]

James Woolsey, CIA Director (*1993 – 1995*), said: "*Assassinations have been clearly illegal under American law since 1975.*" He goes on to say: "*That executive order was signed by President Ford and is still in effect.*" Although the CIA will deny the use of controlled assassins and patsies, one has to wonder if they ever stopped creating them.[80]

Mass Shootings

These events seem to occur more often lately. As higher security measures seem to work in airports, government buildings and even amusement parks, somehow the idea of using the same in schools is not as popular.

---

77 corsair00, "Project Monarch/MK Ultra Victim Mysteriously Taken Off the Air [Coast to Coast AM]," Above top secret, January, 24 2016, accessed August 24, 2017, http://www.abovetopsecret.com/forum/thread1102310/pg1.

78 Gren Whitman, "OPINION: Oswald: "I'm Just a Patsy" — The JFK Assassination Revisited," Common Sense: Straight Talk for the Eastern Shore, last modified Jan 18, 2022, accessed September 5, 2023, https://www.commonsenseeasternshore.org/opinion-oswald-im-just-a-patsy-the-jfk-assassination-revisited.

79 "CIA - MK Ultra - Manchurian Candidates - Controlled Assassins," YouTube video, 59:36, posted by "Proper Gander." January 29, 2017, https://www.youtube.com/watch?v=CvDK7E-6ays

80 "CIA - MK Ultra - Manchurian Candidates - Controlled Assassins," YouTube video, 59:36, posted by "Proper Gander." January 29, 2017, https://www.youtube.com/watch?v=CvDK7E-6ays

What has become popular is the idea of banning certain types of weapons that look like weapons already banned. And some just think the time to do away with guns in the hands of citizens is long overdue.

The tragedy that took place at Sandy Hook Elementary School the morning of December 14, 2012, in Newtown, Connecticut, was one of the most senseless crimes to ever take place in recent history. Twenty children were shot dead between the ages of six to seven, along with six adult staff members.[81] Adam Lanza, the shooter, was also believed to have shot his mother in the head prior to his trip to Sandy Hook Elementary School that day. Classmates described Adam Lanza to have been deeply troubled and fidgety. He had also been diagnosed with Asperger's syndrome, according to family members.[82]

Anti-gun groups rally across the country in support of absolute government control. They don't seem to be interested by the harsh lessons of the past. Most will deny any line of historical fact and continue to repeat the same programmed responses over and over. They go to any lengths to push their point and further their agenda.

Today, they are using *your* children to further their cause. After the mass shooting at **Marjory Stoneman Douglas High School** in *Parkland, Florida* in February of 2018, almost a million students were excused from their classrooms as part of a National School Walkout protest.[83] These kids are now threatening businesses and politicians. And they have made it clear they want to disarm Americans and strip away their 2nd amendment rights. Their claim is that restrictions of *certain* firearms and ammunition will *curb* the number of mass shooting deaths caused by a deranged psycho with a firearm. I admire their ambition and strength; however, I also believe they are *misguided and misinformed*.

California managed to chip away at the 2nd amendment by passing a law that bans high-capacity clips, but a U.S. District Judge blocked it

---

81   Andrew Solomon, "The Reckoning: The father of the Sandy Hook killer searches for answers," The New Yorker, March 17, 2014, accessed August 24, 2017, http://www.newyorker.com/magazine/2014/03/17/the-reckoning

82   Biography.com Editors, "Adam Lanza Biography.com," The Biography.com, A&E Tele- vision Networks, last modified June 13, 2016, accessed August 24, 2017, https://www.biography.com/crime/adam-lanza

83   Jen Kirby, "The March for Our Lives, explained," Vox, March 24, 2018, accessed April 16, 2018, https://www.vox.com/2018/3/19/17139654/march-for-our-lives-dc-march-24-protest.

for now.[84] The city of Deerfield, Illinois passed an "assault weapons and large capacity magazine ban" that includes confiscation. They plan to impose a fine of $1000 per day for gun owners fitting the criteria who refuse to turn them in.[85]

Just the idea of disarming the *law-abiding citizen* to control the criminal should seem *absurd*. Anyone capable of critical thinking, would see the idea of stopping criminals by giving them more laws to break, and disarming their victims as *ridiculous*. Criminals do not abide by laws and they also look for easy targets. Disarming law-abiding citizens will *make* it *much* easier for the criminal to target more victims. This sounds like a law written and sponsored by criminals for criminals. How are so many people blind to the logic to support the gun control agenda?

Unfortunately, so many people have fallen blind to this idea, that making certain firearms and ammunition illegal to own, will solve the mass shooting problem. The politicians and the media use these tragic events to push hard on the need to dismantle people's rights for a false sense of security... and some of the people buy it. Now they are using your children as their foot soldiers. It's time to do some *math*.

Ask Yourself...

Could Adam Lanza have been a Manchurian Candidate, to push the anti-gun campaign?[86] It wouldn't be out of line to think so. How many other senseless mass killings were followed up with a strong push toward the disarmament of American citizens?

Was James Holmes, the 2012 cinema shooter, a Manchurian Candidate? According to eye witness reports, there were *two* killers. Two gas masks were found, and gas canisters were thrown from multiple directions.[87] Among these peculiar bits of evidence, there were other

84 Brandon Morse, "Federal judge blocks California ban on high-capacity magazines," The Blaze, June 30, 2017, accessed September 21, 2017, http://www.theblaze.com/news/2017/06/30/federal-judge-blocks-california-ban-on-high-capacity-magazines/.

85 Steve Pomper, "The Great Gun Grab in Deerfield, Illinois," Opslens, April13,2018, accessed April 16, 2018, https://opslens.com/the-great-gun-grab-in-deerfield-illinois/.

86 "Adam Lanza, James Holmes and Sirhan Sirhan." YouTube video, 6:59, posted by TruthSeeker9Eleven, December 20, 2012, https://www.youtube.com/watch?v=rc3DoeZm09k.

87 "James Holmes Manchurian Candidate MKUltra EXPOSED!!!" YouTube video, 4:56, posted by AMTV, July 30, 2012, https://www.youtube.com/watch?v=aDFVYtJcCbA.

unexplained circumstances that should have warranted further investigation but did not.

Do the Math

After every major event in history, the news media is scrambling to be the first to get the story out. Usually, there are a number of mistakes made, and later reports contradict those that were released prior. After a few months pass, more data begins to surface that tell a better story than the "official" explanation… one that makes much better sense. Something very strange about these recent shooting events was the mysterious deaths surrounding the investigations of them.

27-year-old reporter **Michael Bellmore** *mysteriously* died on May 3, 2014. Bellmore was involved in the earliest reporting on the Sandy Hook shooting event. Along with Bellmore's death, the Connecticut State Police Commander, the Connecticut State Police Commissioner, the Western Connecticut State Police Commander as well as the Connecticut State Medical Examiner, have all been eliminated either by retiring or death.[88]

On April 1, 2018, **Deputy Jason K Fitzsimons** was found dead on his sofa. He was 42 years old and in excellent physical health. His death was officially ruled as *cancer*, but he seemed to have a very active lifestyle, and nobody that knew him mentioned anything about him suffering from cancer. Deputy Fitzsimons was the Broward County Sheriff Deputy who dared to question the official narrative around the Parkland shooting.[89] Why were there *so many* inconsistencies surrounding the shooting event that took place in Parkland, Florida?[90] Also, why are we so quick to accept the official story?

88   Tony Mead, "Sandy Hook's Disappearing Witnesses," Activist Post, last modified July 12, 2014, accessed September 5, 2023, https://www.activistpost.com/2014/07/sandy-hooks-disappearing-witnesses.html.

89   Sean Adl-Tabatabai, "Broward County Sheriff Who Exposed Parkland Shooting Found Dead Media Blackout," The People's Voice, March 2, 2018, accessed September 5, 2023, https://thepeoplesvoice.tv/broward-county-sheriff-parkland-shooting-found-dead/

90   "Parkland Teacher Stacey Lippel Witnessed Parkland Shooter Wearing Metal Garb," YouTube video, 2:56, posted by Philip Stallings, February 25, 2018, https://www.youtube.com/watch?v=dhc9arBKYS0

What Happens in Vegas...

Why isn't anyone investigating what really happened in Las Vegas when too many documented inconsistencies were present surrounding the official story? The **alleged** shooter, **Stephen Paddock**, was a retired accountant. Paddock was a 64-year-old millionaire who owned two planes and several properties across the US. What motive did he have for going on a rampage? Aside from a lack of motive, a bunch of other inconsistencies should have warranted further investigation but *didn't*.

In Vegas there are cameras *literally* <u>everywhere</u>, and yet there's *no footage* of Paddock *anywhere*? This was supposed to be a man in his 60's carrying an arsenal of fully automatic rifles, guns, and ammunition up to his hotel room on the 32nd floor... and *nobody* noticed him? According to CNN, "investigators discovered 23 guns in his hotel room."[91] How many trips would one man need to take from his vehicle to his room, to carry that many firearms and ammunition to go with it? And not one witness noticed this? But more importantly...why would one shooter need that many guns? Police and security radio both confirm multiple shooters on lower floors and halfway up. Victims and eyewitnesses of the shooting also confirmed that there were multiple shooters. One witness stated that exits were closed off, and people were being 'herded'. Before the concert, a lady was warning people in the front, that they were all going to die.

At the hospital, family members of the victims were turned away and told to go to the police station instead... why?[92] Also, like the Sandy Hook shooting event, people that were close to the investigation were silenced before they could blow the lid off what seems to be a cover up story. Eight key witnesses perished in 'questionable conditions' according to WUC News. The report says that each of the eight had something in common besides being present throughout the gunfire:

---

91 Dakin Andone, "The Las Vegas shooter's road to 47 guns," CNN, October 6, 2017, accessed May 10, 2018, https://www.cnn.com/2017/10/06/us/stephen-paddock-47-guns/index.html

92 Emma Cairo, "20 Anomalies regarding the Las Vegas Shooting," Steemit, October 4, 2017, accessed May 9, 2018, https://steemit.com/news/@emmacairo/20-anomalies-regarding-the-las-vegas-shooting

"They each knew details of the massacre which contradicted the 'authorized' narrative. Four of the seven gave accounts to the media which stated there was more than one shooter. Others died before they could speak out."[93]

It All Adds Up

By following the money trail, the real story comes into focus. On **September 5, 2017**, MGM Resorts International announces a share repurchasing program to the tune of one billion dollars. This is usually done to make the stock value go up due to a higher demand.

On **September 7, 2017**, the CEO of MGM dropped 80% of his personal shares in MGM. Why would he do that knowing that the stock prices have a good chance to go up? One theory would be to sell off the shares when they are up, then buy them back when they plummet. Fortunes are made this way. [94] The Las Vegas shooting massacre took place on **October 1, 2017**. No one knows for sure why **James Murren** dumped *so much* of his company's stock when it looked like it was just going *upward* in value. But it would make sense to follow the money trail, because money has been the *motive* for foul play in the past and the present. To get a better scope of the big picture, *independent investigations* will be required for this and every single event like this that has occurred in the past. Allowing government to have the final word is how corruption gets out of control. And when censorship becomes acceptable, and government and media control what you see on the internet, independent investigators and journalists become a high demand.

Censorship in a Free Nation?

Another trend in America that became popular in 2020 was censorship, and on a scale that cannot be missed or denied! Whenever information is

---

93   Admin, "Eight Las Vegas Witnesses Dead Within 30-Days Of Attack," LV Criminal Defense, November 24, 2017, accessed May 10, 2018, https://www.lvcriminaldefense.com/eight-las-vegas-witnesses-dead-within-30-days-attack/

94   @tftproject, "CEO of Company that Owns Mandalay Bay Dumped Massive Amounts of Company's Stock Just Before Shooting," Steemit, last modified October 12, 2017, accessed September 5, 2023, https://steemit.com/conspiracy/@tftproject/ceo-of-company-that-owns-mandalay-bay-dumped-massive-amounts-of-company-s-stock-just-before-shooting.

hidden or removed, it most likely has enough truth to threaten someone to make them want to remove and hide it. What sense would it make to hide bullshit? This video had very interesting highlights that shed light into the Las Vegas Massacre.

https://www.youtube.com/watch?v=97V6BlGr0BA.[95] In 2017, I could view it. In 2021, it was removed. That didn't stop me from digging for it, and with a little thought, came the results. Everything online gets *archived*. The system of surveillance works *both ways. Although I did my best to find what had been buried, there are still social engineers out there deleting articles, video, and other forms of evidence to anything that can incriminate their masters. However, enough evidence has leaked into the hands of the public now in 2023, that people are starting to take a deep look at what has been happening. Censorship in America should wake more people up. Because, when silencing the people becomes the objective, the future is about to get ugly.*

The mass shooting problem we are experiencing here in America today, is due to our *lack of interest* in finding the truth. The purpose for going this far into the details on this topic, is to demonstrate the information that is available, if you really want the facts. Everything is cited. So, feel free to go and look yourself. In fact, that's the point I'm making here. My sources have also cited their sources and so on. Even though some of the

95 VEGAS CASE CLOSED (pt. 2): The Nail In The Coffin!" YouTube video, 11:29, Posted by "Cut2theTruth." Oct 12, 2017. https://www.youtube.com/watch?v=97V6BlGr0BA.

links have changed, with a little digging you will find the data on similar websites. The Internet is a sea of information at your fingertips. It is up to you to do the *fact-checking*.

The only way to truth is to trace everything to its root. The only thing you will find on the surface are the symptoms. The on & off button is buried deep within the subconscious mind... so are the rest of our thinking and behavior patterns and programs.

It's important to understand that if we *can't* get a grip on our own mind, *someone else* has already hacked into it. We are bombarded with digital messages every day. If we are not aware of the constant attack, we will fall victim to it. There is a powerful science being used to control human thinking and consciousness. If they can control what you have access to, they control what you think.

Money-rich people have been in control of the world for way too long. And although the power in numbers favor the other side, their ability to use money to divide the other side has worked well for them. *Psychological warfare* is very powerful science that you should be aware of. There is a very good reason trillions of dollars are spent researching new technology. *Dr. Mengele* would be proud of what science and medicine has become in 2021. The thought of that should worry you.

Social engineers are using ideological subversion to take down a world superpower... with little resistance. This should interest you if you enjoy the freedoms and civil liberties, along with all the creature comforts of the material world. Because life is much different under totalitarian rule. If we sit quietly and accept it, Americans will experience the suffering of many other nations that have lost their freedoms and civil liberties *"for the greater good."*

Ideological Subversion is Psychological Warfare

So here is one final piece of the puzzle that was hard to accept for me at first, but given this mountain of evidence, it's hard to deny. In the past, both Russia and China have said they would take down the US without firing a single shot. How do you suppose that could be done? Well, in

1970, a man by the name of **Yuri Bezmenov**, fled Russia to come here to the US. Mr. Bezmenov was a **former KGB agent** that specialized in *propaganda*. He made it his mission to educate our people about espionage tactics employed by Russia against America.

In these seminars, Mr. Bezmenov referenced a term he called *"Ideological Subversion"* or what he also referred to as *Active Measures* or **psychological warfare.** In a grim interview taped sometime in 1984, Bezmenov mentioned how deeply we were subverted then. In a bone-chilling moment, I got the gist of what I am seeing *today*. He outlines the stealth plan in four stages.

1. First stage is Demoralization.
2. Second stage is Destabilization.
3. Third stage is Crisis.
4. Last and final stage is Normalization.

Demoralization

Signs of demoralization are everywhere. You can see it very clear in the ideas and behaviors of our youth. *"Demoralization is a process to change the perception of reality of every American to such an extent that despite the abundance of information, no one is able to come to sensible conclusions in the interests of defending themselves, their family, their community, and their country."* Bezmenov said, in 1984, by the way. *"This would happen when the 1960s and 1970s student radicals began to control the educational institutions, and their project would be to throw out traditional Judeo-Christian morality, classical education, and American patriotism."* He continued to say. Demoralization takes about 15 – 20 years. This is the minimum number of years to educate one generation of students. And by taking a hard look into our system of education it's clear the process has been working.

Most of our young people today are ignorant of the cultural, intellectual, and philosophical heritage, and some are even ashamed of being American. These people are now in positions of power in the government, civil services, business, mass media, education, and everywhere in between! We are stuck with them!

Psychological warfare makes people feel low, like your civilization is *lost*. Once you succumb to that, you become *satisfied with less*. We can see this attitude in the mainstream and on the street. Everywhere you look people wear a mask, and some wear it on their chin, just to show they have one too. We are seeing signs of demoralization everywhere from our churches to our schools. People inside our government have delusions of power. Instead of administration of the will of the people, some elected officials are in the seats purely for political footing.

Destabilization

Bezmenov describes that as a rapid decline in the structure of a society — its economy, its military, and its foreign relations... and he says this takes between 2 – 5 years to destabilize a nation. It's clear the virus is no longer a significant threat to the health of Americans who don't already have serious medical issues, and yet COVID hysteria is increasing, rather than decreasing.[96] **Scott McKay** saw what I saw in Bezmenov's prediction. "The journalist and Soviet defector long ago pegged the current left-wing moment." McKay brings light to the George Floyd riots among the rest of the chaos. Shutdowns hurt the economy and, in some cases, took out several small businesses that were already struggling. The use of the coronavirus was the perfect platform by which to impose the economic destabilization.

The constant printing of money is not going to remedy the problem either. Anyone who understands finance will agree that our economic collapse is imminent. As for our military, they were among the first to take these new "vaccines" fresh off the assembly line. Nobody really knows what is in them? There isn't a product liability either, so we may never know the damage that will do to our last line of defense, the brave men and women in uniform. Our foreign relations...? Well, that speaks

---

96   Scott McKay, "Four Stages of Marxist Take over: The Accuracy of Yuri Bezmenov," The American Spectator, last modified July 10,2020, accessed April 6, 2021, https://spectator.org/four-stages-of-marxist-takeover-the-accuracy-of-yuri-bezmenov/

for itself. There is an entire book to write on that topic alone. If we take a hard look at where we are, sadly, we are well into this stage.

Crisis

Bezmenov says that a country can be brought to crisis in 6 weeks or less. Once a country becomes demoralized and destabilized, bringing a country into crisis is not difficult. It's like kicking someone when they're down. It is a cowardly move, but that is what we are dealing with here. Only a coward will fight using stealth, and will do it from the shadows.

The events that took place on the morning of September 11, 2001 nearly took the country into crisis. However, the country was not as weak *then*. People pulled together, and the national spirit proved to be strong. This time, the country is much more *divided* and people are much more self- absorbed. The next staged event could easily trigger **Armageddon**... *which is exactly what these psychopaths want.*

Normalization

Normalization happens after a violent change of power structure and economy. This period could last indefinitely. He added: *"Normalization is a cynical expression borrowed from Soviet propaganda. When Soviet tanks moved into Czechoslovakia in 68, comrade Brezhnev said "now the situation in brotherly Czechoslovakia is normalized."*

When we hear the term "new normal" ...could this be the beginning of the *end* of America? One thing is certain, things aren't ever going to be the same again. In terms of normalization, I would say we are seeing signs of this stage too. Violence is becoming the standard and our people are becoming numb to it. There is nothing normal about the things we are seeing and experiencing. Actually, the proper terminology is the *new abnormal*. If we don't snap out of this hypnosis spell quickly, we will regret the consequences.

In Conclusion

As I study the events documented in history, one thing stands out like a stop sign. The turn of events that lead to tyranny are always the same. They occur *in steps*, the ones behind the events are always hidden, and the people about to fall victim never see it coming.

To those who think the loss of our freedoms and gun control are *needed*, seeing how much corruption exists in all levels of government, and how little our government has done in the past to serve its people, ***do you really think your safety and well-being is a priority to them?*** *What if* there really is something more sinister going on? Are you so sure to *gamble* your grandchildren's future on your current beliefs? What if history does repeat because large groups of people are easily led by mind control? How much research have you done on these topics? *And what if you are wrong*?

I ask all of you: *could our government stage the mass murder of its own people, in order to pass anti-gun legislation, and undermine the country's constitutional laws? How many times has this happened before? Where do we draw the line?*

Why didn't the shooting in San Bruno, California on April 3, 2018 raise any outrage from the anti-gun groups?[97] Could it be possible that the female shooter, her choice of weapon, and her motive didn't fit the anti-gun agenda? What about the numerous shooting deaths of criminals at the hand of law-abiding citizens, while committing their crimes? How often do you see that on the news? These questions may sound crazy, but we *must* ask them.

I can continue into *covert missions* and *black operations*, that include *assassinations* of foreign leaders and CIA *coup d'états*. These events happened and involved people who later became high ranking government officials and even former US presidents! They went on to enjoy wealthy lives at the cost of *spilled human blood*...and they did it right in front of your face. Subversion requires the "useful idiot." So, don't be one.

---

97   Robinson Meyer, "What Motivated the YouTube Shooter?" The Atlantic, April 4, 2018, accessed April 16, 2018, https://www.theatlantic.com/technology/archive/2018/04/what-motivated-the-youtube-shooters-terrorism/557237/.

Mind control is a reality. It happens all the time. You may be shocked by this, but now you understand the value of being in control of your own mind. Mind control is administered in many ways, and usually without you knowing. There are more ways for someone to get into your head than there is time to talk about it. Being aware of who's really in control requires you to know a few things and always keep those things in check. It's very important for you to be the one doing the programming. After all, *who else do you want in control of your life?*

Chapter 12:
Reprogramming the
Subconscious Mind

Now that you are aware that reprogramming the mind is possible, the question becomes *how do I do it?* This is the fun part... you already are! Your interest in self-discovery and self-improvement is proof that you are tired of sitting in a dark hole. You're actually looking to change something that doesn't sit right with you. You've come to realize complaining and whining about your problems are useless. And though most people, *myself included*, resort to that first, you have decided to rise above that *this time*.

It's good to be aware that change doesn't begin easily. Keeping the momentum is the key, and should always be the focus. A slow start can turn into a steady pace in a few days, depending on your level of commitment and determination.

Hard work has never killed anyone that I'm aware of. It certainly hasn't killed me yet. And though staying up late and working long hours have drained me of energy from time to time, I always seem to find the power I need to get what I want done, if I really want it bad enough.

As an owner of several businesses, and also a business and life coach, I've noticed too many young people will quit what they are doing when it becomes too difficult for them. They will only show interest in things that are easy and return results instantly. This shows incredible insecurity and weakness.

Having it easy becomes more of a handicap later in life. The most desirable things in life will require you to work hard. Forcing yourself to work hard, and always doing your best, will develop self-control, strength, temperance, and many other virtues, which those that have it easy will never know. These are *character* qualities that are worth working hard to *earn*.

There are many different methods to the reprogramming process. You don't have to stick to only one. In fact, mix it up. Use as many of these methods as it takes for you to gain traction.

Anything the mind can conceive and believe... it can achieve.

Mold Yourself

It's not necessary to copy someone else, but you don't have to reinvent the wheel either. Finding people that have the character qualities you admire is a great first step. Look for things that make you admire these people. You must look *deeper* than their make-up, hair or outfit. The qualities that make people great are found *beneath the flesh*. Remember it's your mind you are wanting to reprogram. It's important that you really question *why* you like this person.

Having a role model, guide, or teacher is the quickest way to get out of yourself and learn new things. When we are stuck in our own way of thinking we are in a hole. Nothing new is going to be found there. The longer we stay in it, the more we miss out on. Role models do not have to be all celebrities either. You may have a parent or a spouse that displays remarkable qualities.

My best friend is someone I admire a lot. Her strength is beyond what I have ever seen, next to my mother's. I admire strong women, and she always displays that. My brother's wit and humor are things I admire. Along with his strength, my brother also has a goofy side that lightens a room when he walks into it.

I admire my dad the most. Here is a man that made a complete change of character late into his 70s! He has proven that you are never too old to change. I have more respect for him, than words can describe. So, you can see just how blessed I am to have so many people with amazing character traits already around me. Although I have my immediate family to mold myself from, I must find more character assets from my much larger family... *the world*.

There are a lot of amazing people that have so much to give the world. The best of them are silenced before their time. It's a shame we couldn't get more time with **Martin Luther King Jr.**, or **John F. and Robert Kennedy**. I wonder how the world would be if these men were to live out their legacy. I wonder how much peace there would be in the world if *Jesus Christ of Nazareth* had been allowed to live to teach Christianity *his way*. What would have become of the *ruling class*? What would have become of *The Church*?

My Mentors

I feel as a recipient of these unlimited blessings in my life, it only makes sense to pass along my findings, and some of my mentors. I want to recommend a few people and some works of literary brilliance that have helped shape my success in life. People have the ability to teach through their words and actions alike. If you only focus on the good one has to offer, you are missing half of the whole. Some teachers are great at teaching the "DON'Ts," and some teach both. It is up to the student to go in with an open mind to learn the lessons *objectively*.

A favorite of all my teachers is **Tony Robbins**. Most people know him right away. Tony has a way with words, that take down walls in my mind. This guy is extremely talented and extremely successful. He is the model that best describes what I want to become. By listening to Tony Robbins and watching him speak, I can gain the knowledge to become who I want to be. His messages are clear and precise, and his techniques are simple and powerful. If you don't know Tony Robbins, or have never heard him speak, I strongly suggest you look him up.

Another great teacher is **Bob Proctor**. If you don't know who this man is, do a search for him. You may recognize him from his self-improvement videos. Bob Proctor is a life coach, and a very good one too. His main area of focus is on the law of attraction, changing your paradigm and reprogramming the subconscious mind. I was first introduced to Bob Proctor by reading *The Secret* by **Rhonda Byrne**.

There are many quotes by this man inside that book. After I watched the movie, I was hooked. Bob Proctor introduced me to another great speaker and author, **Napoleon Hill**. His famous book *Think and Grow Rich*, has been a huge inspiration to me and many other people throughout history. Napoleon's work has helped thousands of people achieve wealth beyond the limit of dreams. Inspired by a suggestion from business magnate and philanthropist **Andrew Carnegie**, Think and Grow Rich can be found in the library of millionaires and billionaires across the world. If you don't have a copy, get one!

Proven Techniques

Like any good student, I had to be ready to try new things. When I was finally ready to experience something else, a teacher came along to guide my way to it. This is how life works. The law of attraction is only one of many natural laws that govern the universe. I explained it well in my book **Higher Powered: A book of Powerful Secrets to Finding Happiness.** Basically, whether or not you believe in the natural laws, they are very real and don't need anyone's approval or validation to work... they just do.

Like the laws of physics, gravity and electricity, these laws work silently in the background and govern the entire universe. To read more on these laws, you can read Higher Powered, or just search for natural laws or universal laws. You will find them quite interesting. Once you understand the laws of nature, everything in life will begin to make better sense. You can also check out the **First Church of Common Sense** (*firstchurchofcommonsense.org*). This sounds funny, but it's actual forgotten theology that is based on *universal laws*. You can also download a **FREE PDF copy** of the book "*Higher Powered*" there. It's worth looking at.

Creativity: The Power of Imagination

One thing that a lot of people don't realize is the power of imagination. This is a success block they place in their own way. Fact be known, we all have the ability to be creative, because we are all creators. Visualization of ideas can prove powerful when applying these techniques to access and reprogram the subconscious mind.

Imagination is something we all had as infants, then as young children, and again as adolescents. Our ideas of how life was going to be were shattered when we became adults and saw the world the way it really was. Then we forgot how to imagine. Our creativity was quickly replaced by practical thinking and cynicism.

We do still have the ability to become more creative, but we need to relax a little and let go of our past beliefs. We need to think like children again. The power of imagination decimates the walls of the mind. Every thought is put together in the workshop of imagination. To live your dreams, you need the ability to dream. This can only be done with a mind that can reach beyond its artificial boundaries.

Autosuggestion

One of the things that **Napoleon Hill** talks about in his book, *Think and Grow Rich*, is autosuggestion. This is feeding your mind. Whatever you feed your mind, becomes your point of attraction. Autosuggestion is a form of self-hypnosis. We do this *unconsciously* most of the time. The untrained habitual form of autosuggestion is what creates what we see as our *problems*. Autosuggestion is so powerful that it works without our knowledge and on its own!

The person that seeks the easy way out of everything is using autosuggestion to set up a *lack* of ambition and will-power in their subconscious mind. What's even worse, this also leads to a state of apathy that results in the loss of self-confidence. The use of autosuggestion to undermine one's own path to success is *very common*. We do this with our best intentions at heart, but our subconscious mind is always going to follow the current paradigm, unless we change it. To change your current paradigm, you must be aware of it, and what you want to change it to.

We can go through life as unconscious sleepwalkers, or take control of the oars, and paddle our way through the river of life. The choice is always ours. Like everything else in nature, autosuggestion isn't magic, it works because science governs it. To activate anything in the subconscious mind, *intense* emotions are required. It's the vibrational energy that turns thoughts into physical reality. There is nothing more powerful than intense emotion to raise your vibrations.

In *Think and Grow Rich*, Napoleon says to write down your autosuggestion on a piece of paper, and he gives specific instruction on how to write it. He also tells you to read it to yourself twice a day, every day. He emphasizes the importance of reading it with emotion. This isn't an easy exercise, but an effective one he says. Anyone that has been able to do it successfully has gone on to find wealth beyond imagination. Napoleon says: "*No thought, whether it be negative or positive can enter the subconscious mind without the aid of the principle of autosuggestion, with the exception of thoughts picked up from the ether.*"

Here is something very important to always keep in your awareness. Autosuggestion is a powerful force of nature. It works effectively either for or against you. Like the forces of water, wind, and fire, autosuggestion can either better sustain your life, or it can take it away.

Affirmations

An affirmation is not to be confused with autosuggestion. When you use affirmations, you are practicing autosuggestion in a deliberate way. You are carefully selecting the dominant thought and allowing it to filter through to your subconscious mind. Affirmations help you overcome negative thoughts and self-sabotage and literally build self-confidence.

In this world, the ability to sell yourself can either open the door to riches, or allow you to experience poverty. Salesmanship is a necessity and it requires an intense level of self-confidence. Affirmations can effectively build self-confidence, if the techniques are willfully applied correctly with faith and emotion.

Although research study has come back inconclusive for its effectiveness, the science behind affirmations is the same as with autosuggestion. Unless you have enough *belief* in the affirmation to feel any emotion, it simply doesn't work by magic. The key here is **intense** *emotion*, at least enough to raise your vibrational energy. You're not going to achieve that going in with flat tires.

The Literal Mind

To use affirmations effectively, you need to first understand how the mind works. Because it processes so much information, the mind takes everything you think and say very literally. It can also take in what others say quite literally too.

Have you ever been insulted by someone and felt hurt by it? For example, if someone calls you a cow, how would that make you feel? Would you feel like a cow? How does the cow feel? Many people would feel hurt by this silly remark. Some would feel fat or huge. They would look for something ugly about the cow to associate themselves with.

How many of us would just laugh, and then think to ourselves, I look nothing like a cow! A cow eats grass all day in a field. A cow has fur and an utter. The average dairy cow weighs about 1500 pounds![98] Our mind takes in what it's fed and is straightforward about the rule of language.

The mind also can't tell the difference between fantasy and reality. This is evident when we watch a scary movie and our mind follows the storyline right into the screen. We may even find ourselves reliving it in a nightmare. Have you ever watched a movie so sad that it made you cry? This is how affirmations work. You must visualize the affirmation to the point of sparking an emotion. Once you do that, the gears go into motion in the subconscious mind and the thought begins to materialize before your eyes.

Positive Transmutations

You reap what you sow. Does this sound familiar? The mind is like a garden. It really has no preference what you plant in it. You can plant edibles or you can plant poison. Either way, it will return to you whatever you plant in abundance.

---

98   The dairy guy, "How much do cows weigh?" Dairy Moos, Aug 18, 2013, accessed May8, 2018,
      http://www.dairymoos.com/how-much-do-cows-weigh/

"I never have any money."
"Everyone hates me."
"I am drowning in debt."
"I can't afford that."
"I feel sick all of the time."
"Life isn't worth living anymore"

These are powerful affirmations, and the emotions that drive these thoughts are even more powerful. The impact that negative affirmations have are just as effective in manifesting into negative experience. It's just as easy to consciously manifest wealth as it is to manifest debt. But because we react to debt with so much negative emotion, believing it to be tangible, the emotions are much stronger. People see wealth as something unobtainable. Therefore, the emotions toward wealth aren't as powerful.

Positive energy has a much higher vibration than negative energy, and that wields more impact on the subconscious mind. Now, think for a moment how much power the opposite of the affirmations above would be if they were driven by the same level of emotion. Feel the emotions when you reaffirm these positive thoughts:

"I always enjoy having lots of money!"
"Everyone enjoys the presence of my company."
"Money does grow on trees."
"I am always in perfect health."
"My life is amazing!"
"I am grateful to be so blessed."

These positive thoughts will transmute any negative energies into positive ones. Planting seeds of positivity and fertilizing it with positive emotions will yield an abundance of the things that bring you more of those positive emotions. Whenever you feel the slightest sign of negative energy, you can change it before it's too late by transmuting it back into positive energy.

"Ask, and it will be given to you; seek, and you will find; knock, and it will be opened to you. For everyone who asks receives, and he who seeks finds, and to him who knocks it will be opened."

—Matthew 7:7-8 New American Standard Bible (NASB)

Definiteness of Purpose

We become and experience what we think about all day long. Strong motive is another vital part of the success process. You must always be very clear as to exactly what you want from life, down to the fine details. If you want money, specify exactly how much money you want and by when you expect it. If you want a nice home, specify what this home will look like and where it will be. Pictures will help visualize your purpose.

I have three vision boards hanging above my desk. I look at them often and visualize myself in those pictures. I can feel the soft carpet in that modern contemporary home I am going to build. I can smell the new car smell in that sportscar in my car gallery. I can feel the warmth in my heart as I help the homeless that need a break in life. I can feel the warm water and the cool breeze from that lagoon I am standing in. This sensory visualization gives me a sense of already being there.

Definiteness of purpose is knowing exactly what you want. This is also where most people fall apart. Most people don't know what they want. People tend to focus more on the things they *don't* want than the things they do want. They are working the ***law of attraction*** backwards. It's no wonder they are getting more of the things they don't want. That's where their focus is all the time

I do everything with a purpose, or I just don't touch it. This exercise keeps me sharp on my game. Purposeful thinking results in a solid direction, and with razor-sharp precision. You can definitely see it in the results. If you want to stand out of a crowd, the one being different is that guy or gal! But, like everything else, it takes awareness and lots of practice.

Consistency

Consistency is sticking to the same principals, process, or pattern of behavior. This is a very important ingredient if you want to see success in anything. If you cannot be consistent, you will eventually falter. Consistency is the foundation of discipline, and the best way into the subconscious mind. When we are consistent, we stay in motion. Momentum is based on the idea that an object in motion stays in motion. In order to move forward, we must keep moving. By building momentum, you are building a powerful force of energy behind your desires that eventually equal the power of a locomotive in full speed. You become unstoppable!

The best way to be consistent is to love what you do. If you dread what you do, you will eventually run out of steam and lose your momentum. When you enjoy what you do, or just enjoy the process, you will not look at anything as being work. Even the most labor-intensive work becomes fun.

My Own Experience

Not too long ago, I was doing landscaping. One of my businesses was a landscape design and build firm that specialized in low maintenance designs. These were unique works of art that used very little water and other resources to stay looking beautiful.

The work was very labor intensive and everything was all about fine details. We removed grass, moved earth, and installed concrete, stone and rock – and we did all of this in 100-degree heat. The conditions were brutal, but the process was like a well-oiled machine. I had my guys follow a sequence that was so well thought out, they enjoyed doing it.

Everyone that stepped onto one of my jobsites noticed how clean everything looked. Even though we were doing a demolition and construction job, everything was cleaned up as we pressed forward. Our process was noticeable to everyone, including the neighbors. This led to more work, higher pay and bigger budgets. Because our process was consistent, so was the high quality of our work. People saw value in that, and the company did very well.

To me, it wasn't a just a job or a paycheck, I really enjoyed doing that. It was landscape art, and I was the artist. In fact, my shirts had "The Artist" embroidered on them. People would see that and say: "Wow... an artist!" I try hard to practice consistency with everything I do now. It is an easy concept to grasp, but getting it to flow is not so easy. I can't emphasize enough how much awareness and practice are needed for it to stick!

I know that once I find a process that works well, that becomes the process I must follow every time. It worked well for the landscape company, and it has worked in every other endeavor before and after that one. Without consistency, you are compromising quality, and the chances you will be doing something over again is high. It's always cheaper doing it right the *first* time... <u>every time</u>.

The Burning Desire

Your desire is a vivid picture of what you want most, or what you want to eventually become in this lifetime. The object of your desire must become an obsession before it will begin to burn. It is only the passionate heat of a burning desire that will be enough to power through those moments of weakness. You will need that kind of tenacity for picking yourself back up. Expect to fall, because you will... but view your falls as a setback and nothing more. Having the right frame of mind is very important to get your desires white hot! The sweetest rewards in life require a fierce climb, so don't expect an easy one. If your approach is strong and you are prepared, nothing will stand in your way.

In the moment of truth, you must be willing to set fire to every way out and press forward. This is what it means to *do or die*. When you leave yourself no possible way to back out, there is only one way to go. If you want to win, allow yourself no retreat. Then, work yourself into a white-heat of burning desire as you press forward. You will win because you gave yourself no other option. Do you possess this kind of courage? If not, then work on that.

You can change any area of the non-physical by using the spirit to drive the mind. A burning desire comes from the core of your being... your spirit. This is why it's such powerful energy. We look at our bodies and feel powerless. Unbeknownst to us, the power we cannot see is lying dormant, waiting for us to discover it! We have been kept in the dark for so long, it's time to come out and see the world from another perspective! My book *Highest Self* explains the difference between the spirit and ego in detail. I recommend it (*obviously*)!

Persistence

Persistence is the follow-through that is needed to get something done. Without this vital element of success, there is no will power. Desire and persistence work together to bring any goal to its fruition. The majority of people will give up when faced with opposition, strife, or resistance. Only a few will press on in the face of all opposition to obtain their goals.

Napoleon Hill uses an analogy that is hard to forget regarding persistence. He says: "*Persistence is to man as what carbon is to steel.*" And "lack of persistence is one of the major causes of failure." He goes on to explain the relationship between desire and persistence. These two work together so close that if your persistence is weak, you need to put more fire under your desires. For it's the heat of your desires that drives your persistence, and your persistence keeps your desires alive.

Enthusiasm

Enthusiasm is like a nitrous oxide fuel injection to a race car. It supercharges your desire into rocket fuel. If you can inspire enthusiasm in yourself, it will rub off on others around you. Enthusiasm is your passion. When you are passionate about what you do, it places a lot more value to the work you do.

Whenever I go on sales appointments, I don't follow a script. Everything I say and do are spontaneous and genuine. I open myself like a book and let my passion convince the client that I am the one to hire. After all, I will be the guy making sure the work gets done as promised. What I have noticed is that those who hire me right away aren't looking to save a few bucks. My pricing is much higher than the average, but then again, the quality of my work justifies it. Employers see this quality as an added bonus to having experience alone. Someone who has knowledge may get the job done but may not be willing to learn anything new. Also, over time this person may become burned out by the day-to-day grind.

Someone who possesses enthusiasm is always eager to do well and learn. When I hired guys for my crew, enthusiasm would get you hired on the spot. In fact, I was more willing to train someone *without* experience that showed the enthusiasm to learn over someone with many years of knowledge.

What I found was interesting. The quality of the workmanship from those I trained myself was much closer to my standards, than those who thought their knowledge alone was good enough for me to accept. The power of enthusiasm is very noticeable and desirable to those looking to hire you. I can say without reservation that your attitude matters. It matters to everyone interacting with you.

Author's Note:

Here is where mind control can work for you: By making positive choices in your thoughts and actions, you will influence others to do the same. Enthusiasm can spread like fire. Loving what you do brings passion to your work. That passion has become my trademark. You can see it in everything I do. Some people are intimidated by it. Most appreciate it. I am who I am, and don't see a need to become someone I'm not.

Being genuine and enthusiastic are great qualities of character to have because they are very rare. But there are other factors to familiarize yourself with. I've been self-employed for most of my adult life and self-educated since *after* high school. Having to depend on yourself for everything is not easy. Because, if you don't do it, it doesn't get done. Learning to rely on myself all of these years was good training for what I am doing now.

Self-Reliance

There is much we can learn from birds. Birds will push their young out of the nest at a certain age. They do this so the young ones can become independent. Birds learn to fly before they hit the ground. This may seem a bit extreme, maybe even cruel, but it's a natural reaction to survive. Birds know when their young are strong enough to use their wings to survive the push out of the nest. It's a shame human haven't figured that out.

Self-mastery occurs when you look for answers from within. You should know that *self-worth* comes from how much you value your intuition. Don't be so quick to accept other people's conclusions. Question everything and think for yourself. Make your own conclusions. One of the greatest qualities to have is *self-reliance*. Our world has become one of mediocrity. Staying true to yourself is necessary if you want you want to rise above "average." True happiness also comes from being self-reliant. Here are some things you can do to strengthen your **Self-Reliance:**

- Take personal responsibility for your own actions.
- Know that you can only change what is yours. And if you point blame outward, know that you're only giving away your power to change the situation.
- Own what's yours... is where you find the power to make the needed changes to suit you better. The good, the bad and the ugly... if it's yours, own it.
- Embrace accountability and always look for your part in any bad situation.
- Don't be embarrassed by a mistake. View mistakes as the building blocks of your character, because that's what they are.

Great leaders are made of this stuff. Now you might be thinking: "*I'm not a leader.*" We *all* are. In order to win at the game of life, you must steer your own ship to your desired destination. Nobody else is going to do that for you. Besides, no one else knows your desires better than *you*!

Plans and Goals

Benjamin Franklin once said: "*If you fail to plan, you are planning to fail.*" Setting goals for yourself is a great way to map out your success plan. You will need to make some adjustments to the plan as you move forward anyway. It is very important to know where you are going. Don't let parents, peers, or anyone else pressure you into their objectives. Personal goals are just that… personal. Mapping out a plan is always a good idea. Setting smart goals is an even better idea. Smart goals are:

Specific
Measurable
Achievable
Relevant
Time Bound

__Smart__ goals are achievable, easy to understand and have a clear point of success. Let's say your goal is "*I want to lose weight.*" That is too vague. How do I win? How much weight is enough? When do I want to see the weight lost? Now apply the acronym and begin to make it a solid goal.

Specific – ask the questions **Who** = Me, **What** = 50 pounds, **When** = 1 year, **Where** = here in my home, & **Why** = to better my health.

Measurable – the 50 pounds answered this question. In this case a number sets a finish line.

Achievable – is 50 pounds of weight loss achievable in twelve months? According to my doctor, yes, it is. If I cut my calorie intake down to 2000 per day, based on my current body weight, I would lose 1 -2 pounds per week. I could potentially exceed my goal.

Relevant – This smart goal fits the why I am doing this. Losing 50 pounds of excess body weight will improve my health. It will give me more flexibility, take a load off of my back, knees, ankles, etc. I will feel better, look better, breathe easier, and be around longer to enjoy the fruits of my labor.

Time Bound – 12-months is a time table for this goal.

So now my goal went **from** *"I want to lose weight"* **to** *"I want to lose 50 pounds in the next 12 months to improve my health."*

I didn't do this in my earlier years. Plans and goals weren't on my list of things to do. I wasted most of my young adult life bouncing. It wasn't until I hit my 30's that setting goals and making plans became a huge part of my process and my success. I don't think I would be where I'm at without adding this step to my process.

Today, I make a choice, set a goal, and then I go all in. I know that to win, I need to give it all of me, and not just a little bit. Luck isn't required when you have a process that works, and you stick to it. Nothing works by magic. Actions that fit the goal is required daily. Setting goals is good practice, because goals are tools. But the tool alone isn't going to win the victory for you. But, your process will.

Rigidness in planning is foolish. Things happen that will require an adjustment to the plan. Order of priority can change. Sequencing is an important element to consider. The idea is to flow from one goal to another, like stepping stones in a path. When your desire becomes white-hot, and your planning flows with the goals, you are in harmony with powerful forces. Then, you become a runaway locomotive – a moving force so powerful, it's unstoppable.

Accurate Knowledge

We live in the age of information, and yet we are starving for knowledge. People pay fortunes to further their education, and yet they only end up with a huge debt they can't pay back. Information is everywhere now, and it's free. The education you can get by just using search engines will render any traditional education *obsolete*. Use your **intuition**. Trusting your gut is very important. Intuition will let you know if something feels right or not. Mine has <u>never</u> let me down. *Has yours?*

Get into the habit of reading. Books are nice, especially non-fiction, because there is a focused topic that has already been researched. I can start with that book and then work off the references and further my research. By the way, it takes years to research and write a decent book…

not a bad deal for ten bucks to the reader! Always remember the power is in the **content** and not *how many* books you read. Always stay focused on the *quality*.

Pick a few books you will read profoundly. I have read **Think and Grow Rich** at least three times already. I will probably read it another twenty more times within my lifetime. That book is worth my time investment. So many others before me have benefited by reading it. Already, I have noticed an improvement in my life as a result of the contents of that *high-quality book*. The author invested his lifetime researching and writing it. I think it would make sense if I invest the rest of mine learning to apply what's in it.

Skills training is always a benefit to self-improvement. I take online classes for everything from improved communication, life coaching, and sales training, to digital marketing, using software, and programming. I even use video tutorials to fix things on my truck and around the house! Online courses are pay-as-you-go and inexpensive. You can amass a decent education for yourself that will improve your life in weeks! Continue your education as you go along, and you will notice your skills becoming stronger and your life experience improving with it.

Focus is Your Outcome

Focus is one area where a lot of humans get tripped up. People put most of their focus on things that offend them, things that they hate, things that they want to see go away. Their focus is heavily on the things that annoy them with boiling emotions. If you are doing this... *stop*.

What you focus on, you will experience. The more your emotions drive those thoughts and ideas, you are actually drawing it to you through the law of attraction. This is a natural law of science. So many people use the law of attraction incorrectly, and then complain about their experience. Most of the time, it's because they don't have a clue that it's working in the background. Here is the greatest power you could ever imagine, and you have full access to it. You can use it to bring your dreams to life or create the experience of hell for yourself.

Think of playing around a nuclear reactor, pushing buttons, and flipping switches randomly, without any knowledge of the consequences. *Is this a good idea?* Any sane individual would read this and say: *"No... hell no!"* That could put you and everyone around you in a hole for good! But we do it anyway, because we don't realize we are doing it *unconsciously*. This behavior is programmed into our framework. Shifting your focus is harder than you think, but it's worth making the effort.

Here is Where it Gets Interesting...
What you focus on, you will eventually come to experience. You are the creator of your experience. Your mind is connected to everything in the universe, and the universe is vast and infinite. Your subconscious mind is also vast and infinite. The only barriers are the ones you create.

Our biggest problem is our lack of focus due to our shortage of attention. We are often carelessly unaware of what is going on around us. I believe this is why people often tend to focus more on the unwanted. Their lack of attention to the wanted shifts their focus to the unwanted. If we are seeking a different reality, our focus is a crucial element and must be pointed at that new reality, in order to create it.

It's important to know there are two ways to focus the mind (toward the positive or the negative), and each way will give you a totally different outcome. It's also very important to be consciously aware of which way we shift our focus to. The subconscious mind will figure out how to create an outcome in either case. The ability to suppress everything unwanted and only focus on the one thing you want is the *key to **life mastery***.

Practice Habit Training
Training the mind to only look at the positive is possible through practice and habit training. Find the positive within any bad experience. Practice that consciously every chance you get. By doing this, you are training your mind to seek out only the positive in every situation. The subconscious mind will learn through conscious repetition and form a new behavior pattern.

Making mistakes through bad habits is something we all do. We continue making the same mistakes over and over because we never acknowledge the mistake for what it is...unacceptable. Our subconscious mind doesn't see the error, so the program continues to run as is. When we justify poor judgment or wrong doings, we are allowing the program to continue. To kill the program, we need to give a clear command to the subconscious that the current program needs to be over-written with _____ (fill in the blank). To do that, we must acknowledge the current program as unacceptable.

Habit training is human intelligence, and it is far more powerful than artificial intelligence. There are people who walk among us that believe AI is the future of humankind. If this is our future, then we are a lot of trouble! Everything requires practice, even just being happy. Happiness is worth the practice. The world maybe going to hell around you, but happiness is also a state of mind. If you want to be happy, you need to learn to let go of being right, and this takes practice.

Focused Repetitive Consistent Practice (FRCP)

Practice makes perfect, right? WRONG. Practice without focus or consistency is a recipe for disaster. As a musician, I had to do a lot of practice in order to send hours of music to memory. For me to perform live, I had to train myself to memorize enough material to take the stage and make what I do look easy. Believe me when I say *it is not!* Performing live without notes requires intense training, and that is how professional touring musicians do it from the rockstars you see in stadiums and arenas to the local and national bands you see at the club level.

Musicians all know rigorous practice involves focus and consistency. If we blow through errors and repeat them, that error is written into the program we are purposely writing into memory. This form of ***habit training*** is very *effective* and results can come *quickly* with concentrated effort!

Understanding Natural Laws

It is a good idea to familiarize yourself with natural laws if you want the best results in mind training. Most of this knowledge has been kept hidden from the general public. Mainly, because a lot of us aren't ready for such powerful information. Only those who seek that level of enlightenment will know what to do with that knowledge. If you are still reading this book and you've come this far, then congratulations! You are certainly interested in life mastery enough to have access to such powerful knowledge, and knowing the world outside and how it relates to the world inside is not only helpful, but _necessary_.

Musicians practice mind training, and many of them aren't even aware that this method can be applied to anything! A lot of computer programmers are just as unaware that they can experience _life mastery_ by applying the same principals that they use to code script to anything else in their life. Learning the **law of correspondence** and other **universal laws** we can achieve the life experience we want! I cover these laws in my book **Higher Powered** and **you can download a FREE copy from my website: Shahryarsadree.com.**

Faith or Fear: Which Will You Choose?

Fear is the killer of dreams and the gatekeeper to our desires. So many people today believe that they are going to remain in poverty because life just handed them that deal. Others have decided to make a career as welfare recipients. Living from hand to mouth has become a way to survive for them. These people can have so much _more_ if they overcome their _fear_. In order to overcome fear, we are going to need _faith_.

The element of faith is what fuels your thoughts with positive emotion, and that by itself will make these new changes stick. Faith can be developed through the consistent use of autosuggestion and affirmations of repeated instructions to the _subconscious mind_.

It's a well-known fact that whatever you tell yourself to believe, _you will_. Even if you think this statement isn't true, if you repeat a lie over and over, eventually you will accept the lie as the truth. **Dominating**

thoughts can direct, guide, and control every movement and action. This is why people are so easily led to believe nonsense and justify the most horrific deeds imaginable. Dominating thoughts can be overwritten in the subconscious, but it will take conscious effort and persistence.

History has shown the world that widespread fear can stop the wheels of industry and bring the economy of a nation to its knees. We've seen this more than once in our own country. It's unfortunate that our entire economy is driven by fear instead of faith.

Think about this for a moment. If the economy is driven by the movement of funds, and the funds keep moving without hesitation or even a pause, wouldn't that build momentum? And wouldn't that result in a stronger economy? After all, *an object in motion stays in motion... right?*

So, if people could just go about their business and have faith that the energy of moving money will keep it moving, *why do we still allow fear to drive our economy?* Even though the laws of science rule the universe, we still allow our fears to blind us from the *facts*.

We all want the same endgame. Freedom, love, and happiness are what all humans seek. It seems we have gravitated toward a culture of fear rather than faith. Even our idea of faith is programmed to be *grossly distorted* and designed to keep us blind, weak, and gripped with fear. If we want a better human experience, it is up to us as individuals to *choose* faith and eliminate the fear. This will improve the quality of our lives, one individual at a time.

Chapter 13:
Endgame – Freedom, Love and Happiness

All humans seek freedom, love, and happiness. I don't care what race, creed, sexual identity, religion or lack of religion you identify with. Everyone is seeking these three things in their own way. It's my observation that the world does not lack these treasures of life that we so desperately seek. In fact, we have become blind to what we are seeking because we place our focus on so many other things we oppose.

We point the blame outward. We look for answers and take comfort from things on the *outside*. It's no wonder why we go *without*. This pattern of human behavior is not natural, but sadly enough, it has become normal. We have found a way to systematically remove the human element from every part of our lives. *Why did we do this, and what purpose does this serve?* The answers are clearly visible if we know where to look.

There was a time when we all had freedom, love, and happiness. Over the centuries, we slowly forgot who and what we are. Now, we all pay to live, while a small group controls all the resources along with the fate of humanity. We lost our perspective in this *grand illusion*. And since perspective is what shapes our reality, our sense of that became the mold for what we are experiencing currently.

If we can look past the multi-racial divide and see ourselves as only *human beings*, we would get a better perspective on how humanity is lost in this superficial existence. Human life has less value than paper and ink in the minds of the many. As institutions took control over the lives of the people, life became meaningless for the many, as they are now labeled the *have-nots* or *mouth-breathers* by the elite who control us. We give them the power to rule over us because we fear their power and aren't aware of our own.

This system of unfair righteousness became our *new normal.* Everyone accepted the terms and went on with their lives. Anyone questioning the logic behind the substitution for politics over science is censored and silenced. We have lost track of what we define as glorious. Instead, we have glorified *wretchedness* and confused THAT with being glorious.

"Through clever and constant application of propaganda, people can be made to see paradise as hell, and also the other way round, to consider the most wretched sort of life as paradise."[99]

— **Adolf Hitler**

Before we can experience freedom, love, and happiness, we need to first explore our path to this confusion. How did we come to this conclusion, and where did we get those ideas, we thought were facts?

The Tower of Power

To get a better understanding of this mystery that has humankind on a leash, we need to take a deeper look at how we got here. Those who established this way of life needed help. There simply aren't enough of them to control the rest of the population. In fact, they are grossly outnumbered. The "1 percent" that we commonly hear about, is really the 0.1 percent. The position of that decimal point makes a huge difference.[100]

There are multiple levels to the *"tower of power."* Below the 0.1 percent, there is the 1 percent. Many of these people work hard at their jobs like the rest of us, and a lot of them contribute to their communities in positive ways. Those at the lower end of the 1 percent, may not even feel rich. Some of them even fear falling off their economic ladder.

Those at the higher end of the 1 percent, and the 0.1 percent, feed and support the political process with their power of money influence.

---

99   "Adolf Hitler > Quotes > Quotable Quote," Good Reads, accessed on March 29, 2021, https://www.goodreads.com/quotes/168242-through-clever-and-constant-application- ofpropaganda-people-can-be.

100   Lynn Stuart Parramore, "The .1 percent are the true villains: What Americans don't understand about income inequality," Salon.com, April 14, 2016, accessed August 26, 2017, https://www.salon.com/2016/04/14/the_1_percent_are_the_real_villains_what_americans_dont_understand_about_income_inequality_partner/.

They buy government officials with their huge contributions to political campaigns. Those television and radio advertisements that go on for years before an election, are mostly funded by these groups. But they also partake in campaign funding and other shady back room deals. This is the reason our laws don't seem just. These groups are also responsible for starting wars and using our military forces for their profit. So, how do they do this, and why isn't anyone stopping them?

Divide and Conquer

The 0.1 percent promote the established system by dividing the people beneath them into smaller and smaller groups. Each group then looks at the other groups as a threat to their own existence. This is the genius behind the plan of "divide and conquer." While the battle is going on between all the have-nots, the focus is taken off those at the very top who are manipulating their established system.

The 1 percent won't question this system, because they still have more than enough to live many comfortable lifetimes. They also fear that if the system is to change in any way, they will lose their position on the economic scale. So, the way things are right now will have to be good enough.

The 1 percent enjoy their monetary wealth growing through capital gains, which is taxed at a much lower rate than income from physical work. In other words, if you trade your labor for dollars, you pay more in taxes than if your money earns more dollars in interest. As you move up to the 0.1 percent ladder, you will see these people doing things like buying preserved dead animal predators as decorations for one of their many homes. Like the hedge fund billionaire who bought a 14-foot shark preserved in formaldehyde... is he trying to make some kind of statement?[101]

101　Alex Marshall, "Shark Woes: Keeping an $8million pickled fish looking tasty," New York Mag.com, February 21, 2005, accessed August 26, 2017, https://nymag.com/nymetro/news/people/columns/intelligencer/11086/

Freedom Is Not Free

The idea of freedom is so far away from its definition, it's like calling a toothbrush a hand bag. The concept of America was once revered around the world. Through our blind support for the enemies within, we have allowed a criminal element to take us back to tyranny. We wave our flags and place stickers on our vehicles that state our support for a system that has no value for human life.

We send our family members into the line of fire and watch as those lucky enough to return, come back physically and psychologically maimed. They are told to deal with their conditions and "*thanks*" for serving *your* country in the name of *freedom*.

Military budgets increase every year, but benefits that are supposed to cover combat veterans are still slow to reach those who gave their lives to serve. The 2018 Defense budget was just under $700 billion.[102] Today, the US has between 700 and 900 military bases in over 80 countries.[103] Some see America as being more imperialism than a nation promoting freedom. According to a Pew Research Center report, more than 50 percent of people in most countries surveyed resent American power, and the numbers continue to rise.[104] Even America's neighbors see the US as more of a threat than Russia or China.[105]

Evil Genius

Most Americans believe whatever they see, read, and hear on mainstream media. This process of indoctrination has made it easy to accept fiction as the truth. This has happened before, if we look back to the pages of history. We are witnessing evidence being buried in real-time, and nobody

---

102 Kimberley Blankenstein, "2018DefenseBudget," MilitaryBenefits.info, accessedMay11, 2018, https://militarybenefits.info/2018-defense-budget-overview/.

103 Thorsten J. Pattberg, "US Imperialism: Timeline of United States Military Operations," Think Big. com, accessed May 11, 2018, https://bigthink.com/articles/us-imperialism-timeline-of-united-states-military-operations/.

104 Guy Raz, "World Sees Imperialism in American Reach, Strength," NPR, November 2, 2006, accessed May 11, 2018, https://www.npr.org/2006/11/02/6423000/world-sees-imperialism-in-american-reach-strength

105 Dorothy Manevich and Hanyu Chwe, "Globally, more people see U.S. power and influence as a major threat," Pew Research Center, August 1, 2017, accessed May 11, 2018, https://www.pewresearch.org/short-reads/2017/08/01/u-s-power-and-influence-increasingly-seen-as-threat-in-other-countries/

is doing anything about it! No public outcry or rage, just business as usual and back to your normal television programming.

Meanwhile... we are kept in the dark when back-room deals are made. Distractions are everywhere you look, and social media platforms make it much easier to spread misinformation and propaganda, while keeping a watchful eye on all of them piss-ants.

The sinister way that keeps the "slaves" thinking that they are free, works flawlessly because nobody asks questions. The oppressed are the ones doing all the dirty work. And they do it to keep themselves in the dark. The plan is brilliant.

Great minds went into creating such a perfect game plan. By hiding one simple secret, they are able to hold down or exterminate the entire population of the planet. Although evil, this level of genius deserves commendation. Being humans, they have proven themselves as the gods. Sheer brilliance. However evil, none-the-less very brilliant.

Most of us cannot think in this direction. It would be like trying to relate to a serial murderer or child rapist. These horrific acts require a capable mind to perform. Most of us aren't equipped for that, so the ability to recognize foul-play is diminished to all but those who commit the crimes, and those who catch criminals. Technology has made it easy for the criminals, but also for the ones who hunt criminals.

The game has taken an interesting turn. Natural selection is trending again. So, we must be on our toes! Mass murder is allowed, but only if it was a vaccine-related murder. The Supreme Court even rules in favor of protecting vaccine makers from product liability. [106] In a very eerie way... we seem to be going back in time. Back to a time when a radical group of over-zealous eugenicist decided to wipe out an entire race. It seems they are back at it again. If we cannot learn from our mistakes from the past, we are doomed to repeat it. The love of power has always led to suffering, because most of us are caught in the middle.

---

106 Thomas Sullivan, "Supreme Court Rules in Favor of Protecting Vaccine Makers from State Lawsuits," Policy & Medicine, last modified May 5, 2018, accessed April 8, 2021, https://www.policymed. com/2011/03/supreme-court-rules-in-favor-of-protecting-vaccine-makers-from-state-lawsuits.html.

The Love of Power

It has been said that *"When the power of love overcomes the love of power, the world will know peace."* Unfortunately, as long as humankind's thoughts are controlled, love and freedom will always elude us. A free-thinking society is a threat to the way of life as we know it. Have you ever stopped to think *why there is so much hatred in our world today?* We are all creatures of light and flesh. At our core, we are pure love energy, the highest form in the universe. We are so powerful that we are able to vibrate into these physical bodies. Have you ever wondered why we are always seeking to love and be loved? Could it be that we are seeking our *source energy* for comfort?

Mankind is in a hole. Your problems are like the dust on a grain of fine sand. The reason your problems seem to be so big, is that you are part of a much larger picture than what you can see. Everything in creation is *one* life entity. People refer to this as *God*.

We choose to be blind. Deep inside, we know the truth but we *choose* to live a life of lies. The secret will remain hidden from all who are not ready to evolve into the next phase of human development. There are those who only want to be miserable and want companionship in that... then there are those who just lost their way. Which one are *you*?

Happiness: The Endgame

This is the most sought-after prize anywhere in the universe. Happiness isn't any particular person, place, or thing, but only a state of mind. It's only the mind that experiences happiness. This is a good thing, because that puts you in charge of finding it and maintaining it.

There are so many people that are conscious to this new revelation, and more awaken every day. You must know that the illusion we believe is real, isn't. Everything is within our mind. You are already a force of love energy. Your light is yours to control. Burn it bright or turn it off, that's your free will.

Nobody can come and take this freedom away from you, unless you freely give it away. Happiness can be obtained when we stop placing expectations on things outside of ourselves. The established system will be what it is until humankind decides it has had enough. As individuals, our power comes from being aware and being open to new ideas. There are plenty in this book. Happiness is a personal choice. You can live down in a hole or find your mountain top.

Life is a dream; it is yours to realize.

BIBLIOGRAPHY

@tftproject. "CEO of Company that Owns Mandalay Bay Dumped Massive Amounts of Company's Stock Just Before Shooting," Steemit. October 12, 2017. Accessed September 5, 2023. https://steemit.com/conspiracy/@tftproject/ceo-of-company-that-owns-mandalay-bay-dumped-massive-amounts-of-company-s-stock-just-before-shooting

ABC 10 News, "Pelosi admits to using "wrap up smear?" YouTube video, 0:52, October 10, 2018. https://www.youtube.com/watch?v=WzA-V_1lk40.

Adl-Tabatabai, Sean. "Broward County Sheriff Who Exposed Parkland Shooting Found Dead – Media Blackout," YourNewsWire.com. Last modified April 13, 2018. Accessed May 8, 2018. https://yournewswire.com/broward-county-sheriff-parkland-shooting-found-dead/.

Admin. "Eight Las Vegas Witnesses Dead Within 30-Days Of Attack." LV Criminal Defense. Last modified November 24, 2017. Accessed May 10, 2018. https://www.lvcriminaldefense.com/eight-las-vegas-witnesses-dead-within-30-days-attack/.

Alexiou, Gus. "Website Accessibility Lawsuits Rising Exponentially In 2023 According To Latest Data," Forbes. Jun 30, 2023. Accessed Sept 5, 2023, https://www.forbes.com/sites/gusalexiou/2023/06/30/website-accessibility-lawsuits-rising-exponentially-in-2023-according-to-latest-data/?sh=441b8805717f.

Ameen, Luke. "The 25 Scariest Texting and Driving Accident Statistics," ICEBIKE. Accessed August 5, 2016. http://www.icebike.org/texting-and-driving/.

AMTV "James Holmes Manchurian Candidate MKUltra EXPOSED!!!" YouTube video. 4:56. July 30, 2012. https://www.youtube.com/watch?v=aDFVYtJcCbA.

Andone, Dakin. "The Las Vegas shooter's road to 47 guns," CNN. Last modified October 6, 2017. Accessed May 10, 2018. https://www.cnn.com/2017/10/06/us/stephen-paddock-47-guns/index.html.

Baran, Nicole. "Barriers to Leaving an Abusive Relationship," Center for Relationship Abuse Awareness. Accessed: August 7, 2017. http://stoprelationshipabuse.org/educated/barriers-to-leaving-an-abusive-relationship/.

Barrow, Courtney "Centralia, Pennsylvania: How an underground mine fire turned a thriving community into an eerie ghost town," AccuWeather. March 31, 2017. Accessed June 20, 2017. https://www.accuweather.com/en/weather-news/ghost-town-explored-centralias-mine-fire-smolders-300-feet-below-an-eerie-abandoned-landscape/70001172.

Bendix, Aria. "High levels of a hazardous chemical polluted the air weeks after the Ohio train derailment, an analysis shows," NBC Health News. July 12, 2023. Accessed September 1, 2023, https://www.nbcnews.com/health/health-news/ohio-train-derailment-hazardous-chemical-polluted-air-rcna93640.

Biography.com Editors. "Adam Lanza Biography.com," The Biography.com. A&E Television Networks. last modified June 13, 2016. Accessed August 24, 2017. https://www.biography.com/people/adam-lanza-21068899.

Biography.com Editors. "Ludwig van Beethoven Biography," The Biography.com. A&E Television Networks. Last updated April 27, 2017. Accessed August 7, 2017. https://www.biography.com/people/ludwig-van-beethoven-9204862.

Biography.com Editors. "Mahatma Gandhi Biography.com," The Biography.com website. A&E Television Networks. Last updated August 4, 2017. Accessed August 29, 2017, https://www.biography.com/people/mahatma-gandhi-9305898.

Biography.com Editors. "Michael Jordan Biography," The Biography.com. A&E Television Networks. Last updated August 1, 2017. Accessed August 7, 2017. https://www.biography.com/people/michael-jordan-9358066.

Biography.com Editors. "Rosa Parks Biography.com," The Biography.com website. A&E Television Networks. Last updated August 7, 2017. Accessed August 29, 2017. https://www.biography.com/people/rosa-parks-9433715.

Biography.com Editors. "Thomas Edison Biography," The Biography.com. A&E Television Networks. Last updated August 4, 2017. Accessed August 7, 2017. https://www.biography.com/people/thomas-edison-9284349.

Biography.com Editors. "Walt Disney Biography," The Biography.com. A&E Television Networks. Last updated August 7, 2017. Accessed August 7, 2017. https://www.biography.com/people/walt-disney-9275533.

Bland, Scott. "Julian Assange: the hacker who created WikiLeaks," The Christian Science Monitor. Last modified July 26, 2010. Accessed May 14, 2018, https://www.csmonitor.com/USA/Military/2010/0726/Julian-Assange-the-hacker-who-created-WikiLeaks.

Blankenstein, Kimberley. "2018 Defense Budget," Military Benefits.info. Accessed May 11, 2018. https://militarybenefits.info/2018-defense-budget-overview/.

Blevins, Melissa. "Project Mkultra: One of the Most Shocking CIA Programs of All Time," Gizmodo. September 23, 2013. Accessed August 21, 2017. http://gizmodo.com/project-mkultra-one-of-the-most-shocking-cia-programs-1370236359.

Cairo, Emma "20 Anomalies regarding the Las Vegas Shooting," Steemit. Last modified October 4, 2017. Accessed May 9, 2018. https://steemit.com/news/@emmacairo/20-anomalies-regarding-the-las-vegas-shooting.

Calamur, Krishnadev. "Australia's Lessons on Gun Control," The Atlantic. Last modified October 2, 2017. Accessed May 14, 2018. https://www.theatlantic.com/international/archive/2017/10/australia-gun-control/541710/.

Canfield, Kevin. "The Sinister Scientist Behind the CIA's Mind-Control Mayhem," Daily Beast. November 30, 2019. Accessed September

5, 2023, https://www.thedailybeast.com/the-sinister-scientist-behind-the-cias-mind-control-mayhem.

Cherry, Kendra. "What Is the Conscious Mind?" Verywell.com. Last modified June 16, 2016. Accessed August 10, 2017. https://www.verywell.com/what-is-the-conscious-mind-2794984.

Clements, Erin. "Woman who inspired 'It's My Party' reveals story behind the song's catchphrase," Today.com. Last modified Feb. 20, 2015. Accessed April 2, 2017. http://www.today.com/popculture/lesley-gores-its-my-party-story-behind-song-t4291.

Cohen, Jennifer. "5 Proven Methods for Gaining Self Discipline," Forbes. June 18, 2014. Accessed August 9, 2017. https://www.forbes.com/sites/jennifercohen/2014/06/18/5-proven-methods-for-gaining-self-discipline/#f7ab62b3c9f8

Collins, Sam P.K. "Americans to the Emergency Room Every Year," Think Progress. October 10, 2014. Accessed August 10, 2016. https://thinkprogress.org/car-accidents-send-2-5-million-americans-to-the-emergency-room-every-year-b81b191a09b8/.

Corsair00. "Project Monarch/MK Ultra Victim Mysteriously Taken Off the Air [Coast to Coast AM]," Abovetopsecret. January, 24 2016. Accessed August 24, 2017. http://www.abovetopsecret.com/forum/thread1102310/pg1.

Cut2theTruth. "VEGAS CASE CLOSED (pt. 2): The Nail In The Coffin!" YouTube video, 11:29. Oct 12, 2017. https://www.youtube.com/watch?v=97V6BlGr0BA.

Dagalagas, "Joe Biden Brags about getting Ukranian Prosecutor Fired." YouTube video, 1:15, posted by September 20, 2019. https://www.youtube.com/watch?v=UXA--dj2-CY.

Deflin, Kendall. "10 Things You Never Knew About Stevie Wonder," Live for Live Music. May 13, 2017. Accessed August 7, 2017. http://liveforlivemusic.com/features/10-things-stevie-wonder/.

Doctor, Mark "Wrong Way Driving: New Focus on a Persistent Problem," TRB Webinar, Federal Highway Administration Resource

Center, April 20, 2016. Accessed January 3, 2017. http://onlinepubs. trb.org/Onlinepubs/webinars/160420.pdf.

Duffy, Tony. "Caitlyn Jenner's transformation," CBS News. Accessed August 3, 2017. http://www.cbsnews.com/pictures/bruce-jenner-over-the-years/.

DR. Malik Burnett and Amanda Reiman, PHD, MSW. "How Did Marijuana Become Illegal in the First Place?" Drug Policy Alliance. October 8, 2014. Accessed May 10, 2018. http://www.drugpolicy.org/blog/how-did-marijuana-become-illegal-first-place.

"Drug Scheduling." United States Drug Enforcement Administration. Accessed May 10, 2018. https://www.dea.gov/druginfo/ds.shtml

Eldrige, Lynne, MD. "Overview and Types of Hypoxia." Verywell Health. Last modified November 19, 2020. Accessed April 6, 2021. https://www.verywellhealth.com/hypoxia-types-symptoms-and-causes-2248929.

Elkins, Chris. "Hooked on Pharmaceuticals: Prescription Drug Abuse in America," DrugWatch. Last modified July 29, 2015. Accessed April 5, 2017. https://www.drugwatch.com/2015/07/29/drug-abuse-in-america/.

EMS1 Staff, "What are crisis actors?," EMS1, May 4, 2018, accessed April 5, 2021, https://www.ems1.com/mass-casualty-incidents-mci/articles/what-are-crisis-actors-9DwQ3kdMYgUo66wp/

Evans, Jules. "How ancient philosophy saved my life," Philosophy For Life. May 8, 2012. Accessed May 3, 2017. http://www.philosophyforlife.org/times-piece-on-ancient-philosophy-cbt-and-the-politics-of-well-being/.

Feloni, Richard and Lutz, Ashley. "23 Incredibly Successful People Who Failed at First," Business Insider. March 7, 2014. Accessed August 7, 2017. http://www.businessinsider.com/successful-people-who-failed-at-first-2014-3/#nston-churchill-was-estranged-from-his-political-party-over-ideological-disagreements-during-the-wilderness-years-of-1929-to-1939-1.

Freedom Taxi. "Self Discipline, A Great Audio Book." YouTube video, 4:12:54. August 30, 2016. https://www.youtube.com/watch?v=1SixH8C_1I4.

Gavin, Philip. "The Rise of Adolf Hitler." The History Place. 1996. Accessed August 23, 2017. http://www.historyplace.com/worldwar2/riseofhitler/party.htm.

Gearino, Dan. "California Just Banned Gas-Powered Cars. Here's Everything You Need to Know," Inside Climate News. September 1, 2022. Accessed September 1, 2023. https://insideclimatenews.org/news/01092022/california-just-banned-gas-powered-cars-heres-everything-you-need-to-know/

Gorrey, Megan. "Top 10 excuses ACT drivers use to get out of speeding fines," ACT News. August 11, 2014. Accessed August 28, 2016. http://www.canberratimes.com.au/act-news/top-10-excuses-act-drivers-use-to-get-out-of-speeding-fines-20140805-100p4t.html

Guidance 2222. "Julian Assange? & The Anne Hamilton-Byrne Cult Rumour." YouTube video, May 19, 2017, 40:34. https://www.youtube.com/watch?v=UcdhMSgZAHM.

Guterl, Fred. 2020. "Dr. Fauci Backed Controversial Wuhan Lab with U.S. Dollars for Risky Coronavirus Research." Newsweek. April 28. Accessed March 18, 2021. https://www.newsweek.com/dr-fauci-backed-controversial-wuhan-lab-millions-us-dollars-risky-coronavirus-research-1500741?fbclid=IwAR0wf7e7ifeE7QPUqeUOs9SlzgY12QveTz4wSNH3exBSK1Gvq70jJqWW_uU.

Haines, Stephanie. "Report: Cell phone distraction causes one in four US car crashes," The Christian Science Monitor. January 12, 2010. Accessed August 10 2016. https://www.csmonitor.com/USA/2010/0112/Report-Cell-phone-distraction-causes-one-in-four-US-car-crashes.

Hayward, Rebecca. "NEW BREAKING NEWS Julian ASSANGE & MK Ultra Project Monarch & WIKILEAKS Founder Beginnings (HOT)." YouTube video, December 9, 2016, 50:39. https://www.youtube.com/watch?time_continue=210&v=WlKFz5l9MNU.

Hazelden Betty Ford Foundation. "Substance Abuse Among the Elderly a Growing Problem," Hazelden Betty Ford Foundation. Last modified May 11, 2015. Accessed April 5, 2017. http://www.

hazeldenbettyford.org/articles/substance-abuse-among-the-elderly-a-growing-problem.

Henderson, Mary. "Subconscious Mind – How To Reprogram Your Subconscious Mind." YouTube video, 8:41. August 27, 2014. https://www.youtube.com/watch?v=ibet0kpKQvM.

Hill, Napoleon. Think and Grow Rich. Meriden, CT: The Ralston Society 1938. OpportunityInformer.com

Hiskey, Daven. "The American Government Once Intentionally Poisoned Certain Alcohol Supplies Resulting in the Death of Over 10,000 American Citizens," Today I Found Out. July 30, 2010. Accessed August 27, 2017. http://www.todayifoundout.com/index.php/2010/07/the-american-government-once-intentionally-poisoned-certain-alcohol-supplies-resulting-in-the-death-of-over-10000-american-citizens/.

History.com Staff. "History of MK-Ultra." History.com. A+E Networks. 2017. Accessed August 21, 2017. http://www.history.com/topics/history-of-mk-ultra.

History.com Staff. "KKK Founded." History.com. A+E Networks. 2010. Accessed August 23, 2017. http://www.history.com/this-day-in-history/kkk-founded.

Holmes, Marian Smith "The Freedom Riders, Then and Now," Smithsonian.com. February 2009. Accessed August 29, 2017. http://www.smithsonianmag.com/history/the-freedom-riders-then-and-now-45351758/.

Improvement Pill. "How to Brainwash Yourself to Succeed – Affirmations." YouTube video, 10:42. April 13, 2017. https://www.youtube.com/watch?v=1F7GP9mKkiM.

Inter-Pathé. "Reefer Madness (1936)." YouTube video, 1:08:18. April 10, 2015. https://www.youtube.com/watch?v=zhQlcMHhF3w.

Jacobsen, Annie. "Operation Paperclip: The Secret Intelligence Program to Bring Nazi Scientists to America," Central Intelligence Agency. Last modified Oct 06, 2014. Accessed May 11, 2018. https://www.cia.gov/library/center-for-the-study-of-intelligence/csi-publications/csi-studies/studies/vol-58-no-3/operation-paperclip-the-secret-intelligence-program-to-bring-nazi-scientists-to-america.html.

Jewish Virtual Library. "Israel Military Intelligence: The Lavon Affair (Summer 1954)," Accessed August 24, 2017. http://www.jewishvirtuallibrary.org/the-lavon-affair.

Kardaras Ph.D., Nicholas. "The Ancient Greek Cure for Depression and Anxiety," Psychology Today. Last modified May 27, 2011. Accessed April 15, 2017. https://www.psychologytoday.com/blog/how-plato-can-save-your-life/201105/the-ancient-greek-cure-depression-and-anxiety.

Kirby, Jen. "The March for Our Lives, explained," Vox.Last modified March 24, 2018. Accessed April 16, 2018. https://www.vox.com/2018/3/19/17139654/march-for-our-lives-dc-march-24-protest.

Kelly, Kate. "Remember Duck and Cover? What Safety Experts May Have Been Thinking," Huffington Post. Last modified May 25, 2011. Accessed August 21, 2017. http://www.huffingtonpost.com/kate-kelly/remember-duck-and-cover-w_b_774134.html.

KTAR. "More than 1,600 wrong-way driving incidents reported in Arizona," KTAR News. Last modified December 14, 2016. Accessed January 3, 2017. https://ktar.com/story/1390272/arizona-dps-over-1600-wrong-way-driving-incidents-reported-to-dps-this-year/.

Law of Attraction Coaching. "Jim Rohn: Self Discipline." YouTube video, 41:44. June 15, 2017. https://www.youtube.com/watch?v=KFpe8X4knD8.

Law of Attraction Coaching. "Tony Robbins: SELF DISCIPLINE (Motivational Video)". YouTube video, 22:48. October 10, 2016. https://www.youtube.com/watch?v=51UQl9xm23Q.

Leonard, Jerry. "The "Manchurian Candidate": Lee Harvey Oswald?" Accessed September 21, 2017. http://www.winstonsmith.net/mancurian%20candidate%20longer%20version%20ezine.htm.

Lewis, Sophie. "Joe Biden breaks Obama's record for most votes ever cast for a U.S. presidential candidate," CBS News, Last modified December 7, 2020. accessed March 28, 2021. https://www.cbsnews.

com/news/joe-biden-popular-vote-record-barack-obama-us-presidential-election-donald-trump/.

Lichtblau, Eric. "Nazis Were Given 'Safe Haven' in U.S., Report Says," The New Your Times. Last modified November 14, 2010. Accessed May 11, 2018. https://www.nytimes.com/2010/11/14/us/14nazis.html.

MacQueen, Dr. Graeme. "118 Witnesses: The Firefighters' Testimony to Explosions in the Twin Towers." 2500+ Architects & Engineers for 9/11 Truth. Last modified August 21, 2006. Accessed May 8, 2018. https://www.ae911truth.org/evidence/technical-articles/articles-in-the-journal-of-9-11-studies/112-118-witnesses-the-firefighters-testimony-to-explosions-in-the-twin-towers.

Manevich, Dorothy, and Hanyu Chwe. "Globally, more people see U.S. power and influence as a major threat," Pew Research Center. Last modified August 1, 2017. Accessed May 11, 2018. http://www.pewresearch.org/fact-tank/2017/08/01/u-s-power-and-influence-increasingly-seen-as-threat-in-other-countries/.

Margolis, Mac. "Ecuador Wants Less Julian Assange and More Foreign Investors," Bloomberg. Last modified April 5, 2018. Accessed May 14, 2018. https://www.bloomberg.com/view/articles/2018-04-05/ecuador-wants-less-assange-and-more-foreign-investors.

Marshall, Alex. "Shark Woes: Keeping an $8 million pickled fish looking tasty," New York Mag.com. Last modified February 21, 2005. Accessed August 26, 2017. http://nymag.com/nymetro/news/people/columns/intelligencer/11086/.

McKay, Scott. "Four Stages of Marxist Takeover: The Accuracy of Yuri Bezmenov." The American Spectator. Last modified July 10, 2020. Accessed April 6, 2021. https://spectator.org/four-stages-of-marxist-takeover-the-accuracy-of-yuri-bezmenov/.

Mielach, David. "5 Business Tips from Albert Einstein," BusinessNewsDaily. Last modified April 18, 2012. Accessed March 11, 2018. https://www.businessnewsdaily.com/2381-albert-einstein-business-tips.html.

Mead, Tony. "Sandy Hook's Disappearing Witnesses." Memoryhole Blog. Last modified July 10, 2014. Accessed May 8, 2018. http:// memoryholeblog.org/2014/07/10/sandy-hook-massacres-disappearing-witnesses/.

Meyer, Robinson. "What Motivated the YouTube Shooter?" The Atlantic. Last modified April 4, 2018. Accessed April 16, 2018. https:// www.theatlantic.com/technology/archive/2018/04/what-motivated-the-youtube-shooters-terrorism/557237/.

MLA style. "Martin Luther King Jr. - Biography". Nobelprize.org. Nobel Media AB 2014. Accessed August 29, 2017. http://www.nobelprize. org/nobel_prizes/peace/laureates/1964/king-bio.html.

Moran, Sean. "Asked About Failing Cities by Tucker Carlson, Pence Says 'Not My Concern," Breitbart. July 14, 2023. Accessed September 7, 2023. https://www.breitbart.com/politics/2023/07/14/mike-pence-says-crumbling-cities-not-my-concern-as-he-calls-for-more-aid-to-ukraine/.

Morse, Brandon. "Federal judge blocks California ban on high-capacity magazines," The Blaze. June 30, 2017. Accessed September 21, 2017. http://www.theblaze.com/news/2017/06/30/federal-judge-blocks-california-ban-on-high-capacity-magazines/.

Newton, Terence "13-Year-Old Invents Tesla Inspired Free Energy Device for Under $15," Waking Times. May 18, 2016. Accessed August 7, 2017. http://www.wakingtimes.com/2016/05/18/13-year-old-invents-tesla-inspired-free-energy-device-for-under-15/.

Norberry, Jennifer, Derek Woolner, and Kirsty Magarey. "After Port Arthur - Issues of Gun Control in Australia," Parliament of Australia. Current Issues Brief 16 1995-96. Accessed May 14, 2018. https:// www.aph.gov.au/About_Parliament/Parliamentary_Departments/ Parliamentary_Library/Publications_Archive/CIB/cib9596/96cib16.

Parramore, Lynn Stuart. "The .1 percent are the true villains: What Americans don't understand about income inequality," Salon.com. Last modified April 14, 2016. Accessed August 26, 2017. https://www. salon.com/2016/04/14/the_1_percent_are_the_real_villains_what_ americans_dont_understand_about_income_inequality_partner/.

Pattberg, Thorsten J. "US Imperialism: Timeline of United States Military Operations," Think Big.com. Accessed May 11, 2018. http://bigthink.com/dragons-and-pandas/us-imperialism-timeline-of-united-states-military-operations.

Pema Dechen Rapten. "The Rise of the Nazi Party, 1933." Mount Holyoke College. (n.d.). Access August 23, 2017. https://www.mtholyoke.edu/~rapte22p/classweb/interwarperiod/naziparty.html.

Pomper, Steve. "The Great Gun Grab in Deerfield, Illinois," Opslens. Last modified April 13,2018. Accessed April 16, 2018. https://www.opslens.com/2018/04/13/the-great-gun-grab-in-deerfield-illinois/.

Proctor Gallagher Institute. "How to Change a Paradigm." YouTube video, 12:34. April 23, 2015. https://www.youtube.com/watch?v=IOn3Ay0Uiio.

Proctor Gallagher Institute. "Paradigm Shift: An In Depth Explanation." YouTube video, 27:44. April 14, 2016. https://www.youtube.com/watch?v=z2IEiYM_iYM.

Proper Gander. "CIA - MK Ultra - Manchurian Candidates - Controlled Assassins." You Tube video. 59:36. January 29, 2017. https://www.youtube.com/watch?v=CvDK7E-6ays.

Radwan, M.Farouk, MSc. "Conscious vs Subconscious Mind," 2know myself.com. Accessed August 10, 2017. https://www.2knowmyself.com/subconscious_mind/conscious_mind_vs_subconscious_mind

Raz, Guy. "World Sees 'Imperialism' in American Reach, Strength," NPR. Last modified November 2, 2006. Accessed May 11, 2018. https://www.npr.org/templates/story/story.php?storyId=6423000.

Reallygraceful. "Conspiracy THEORIES Turned Conspiracy FACTS that Change Everything (2017)." YouTube video November 7, 2017, 11:51. https://www.youtube.com/watch?v=6t5tr8IRWfU.

Reallygraceful. "Operation Paperclip & Its Consequences | Explained in 5 Minutes." YouTube video February 24, 2017, 5:13. https://www.youtube.com/watch?v=CNsZQsXxqOM.

Reallygraceful. "What the Media Won't Tell You About Iran." YouTube video November 22, 2017, 11:56. https://www.youtube.com/watch?v=xH9PVkdwjrg.

Roadside America Team. "Centralia Mine Fire," RoadsideAmerica.com. Accessed June20, 2017. http://www.roadsideamerica.com/story/2196.

Salzberg, Steven. "Gain-Of-Function Experiments At Boston University Create A Deadly New Covid-19 Virus. Who Thought This Was A Good Idea?". Forbes. Oct 24, 2022. Accessed September 1, 2023. https://www.forbes.com/sites/stevensalzberg/2022/10/24/gain-of-function-experiments-at-boston-university-create-a-deadly-new-covid-19-virus-who-thought-this-was-a-good-idea/?sh=6533d4b55ca3.

Sasson, Remez. "Self Discipline Benefits and Importance," Success Consciousness. Accessed: August 9, 2017. http://www.successconsciousness.com/self_discipline.htm.

Sebastain Edward, "MK-Ultra Project, Monarch and Julian Assange," Medium, January 19, 2015, accessed May 11, 2018, https://medium.com/@sebastianedward/mk-ultra-project-monarch-and-julian-assange-ad2aa42ba1a4.

Seddon, Keith H. "Epictetus (55–135 C.E.)," Internet Encyclopedia of Philosophy. 2014. Accessed May 12, 2017, http://www.iep.utm.edu/epictetu/.

Seddon, Keith H. "Epictetus (55–135 C.E.)," Internet Encyclopedia of Philosophy. 2014. Accessed May 12, 2017, http://www.iep.utm.edu/epictetu/.

Solomon, Andrew. "The Reckoning: The father of the Sandy Hook killer searches for answers," The New Yorker. March 17, 2014. Accessed August 24, 2017. http://www.newyorker.com/magazine/2014/03/17/the-reckoning.

SourceFedNERD, "The Force Explained - Star Wars 101." YouTube video, 5:38. Oct 17, 2015. https://www.youtube.com/watch?v=539SUcTrhDk.

Spike1138. "Who Exactly is "Julian Assange"..?" News Spike. Last modified June 29, 2013. Accessed May 14, 2018. http://spikethenews. blogspot.com/2013/06/who-exactly-is-assange.html.

Struyk, Ryan. "By the numbers: 7 charts that explain hate groups in the United States." CNN. Updated August 15, 2017. Access August 23, 2017. http://www.cnn.com/2017/08/14/politics/charts-explain-us-hate-groups/index.html.

Sullivan, Thomas. "Supreme Court Rules in Favor of Protecting Vaccine Makers from State Lawsuits." Policy & Medicine. Last modified May 5, 2018. Accessed April 8, 2021. https://www.policymed.com/2011/03/supreme-court-rules-in-favor-of-protecting-vaccine-makers-from-state-lawsuits.html.

Sydney Morning Herald. "Possible police role in 2002 Bali attack," October 12, 2005. accessed August 24, 2017. http://www.smh.com.au/news/National/Possible-police-role-in-2002-Bali-attack/2005/10/12/1128796591857.html.

Taylor, C., Colgan, S. Regulation of immunity and inflammation by hypoxia in immunological niches. Nat Rev Immunol 17, 774–785 (2017). https://doi.org/10.1038/nri.2017.103

Texas Liberty Advocate Network Action. "Josef Mengele - Nazi Third Reich Darwinian Scientific Racism - Eugenics – Depopulation." YouTube video, December 13, 2017. https://www.youtube.com/watch?v=onw-W5uGz1w.

The dairy guy. "How much do cows weigh?" Dairy Moos. Last modified Aug 18, 2013. Accessed May 8, 2018. http://www.dairymoos.com/how-much-do-cows-weigh/.

The Event Is coming soon. "The Trinity of Mind – The Conscious, Subconscious, and Unconscious." YouTube video, 8:39. February 10, 2017. https://www.youtube.com/watch?v=aw600ulIhQ4.

TheLipTV. "MK ULTRA Sleeper Assassin Confession: Government Scopolamine Secrets." You Tube video. 54:27. August 30, 2015. https://www.youtube.com/watch?v=Sau-pI_OI3o.

"The Reichstag Fire," Holocaust Encyclopedia. United States Holocaust Memorial Museum. (n.d.). Accessed August 24, 2017. https://www.ushmm.org/wlc/en/article.php?ModuleId=10007657.

Tongol, Joshua. "How to CREATE and BEND REALITY (You Can Actually Do This!)." YouTube video, 15:56. March 1, 2017. https://www.youtube.com/watch?v=KJYqb6PsOqE.

Torrez, Don. "The Real Reason Local Governments are Facing More ADA Non-Compliance Fines." Governing the future of states and localities. Last modified March 15, 2019. Accessed April 5, 2021. https://www.governing.com/archive/The-Real-Reason-Local-Governments-are-Facing-More-ADA-Non-Compliance-Fines.html.

Traffic Safety Facts. "2015 Motor Vehicle Crashes: Overview," U.S. Department of Transportation. National Highway Traffic Safety Administration. Last revised August 2016. Accessed August 28, 2017. https://crashstats.nhtsa.dot.gov/Api/Public/ViewPublication/812318.

Turkish Daily News. "Court says senior officers involved in Semdinli bombing," Last modified January 5 2008. Accessed August 24, 2017. http://www.wanttoknow.info/documents/false_flag_turkey.htm.

Vialls, Joe. "Lack of Forensic Evidence at Port Arthur," Love for Life. Last modified November 16, 1997. Accessed May 14, 2018. http://loveforlife.com.au/content/08/07/30/lack-forensic-evidence-port-arthur-joe-vialls-sergeant-gerard-dutton-officer-charge.

Wade, Therese. "Nikola Tesla," Antara Healing Arts. March 27, 2016. Accessed August 7, 2017. https://antarahealingarts.com/tag/nikola-tesla.

WantToKnow.info Staff. "False Flag: Summary of False Flag Operations and False Flag Terrorism," WantToKnow.info. Accessed August 24, 2017, http://www.wanttoknow.info/falseflag.

Warrell, Margie. "Find Your Courage: 12 Everyday Acts of Courage to Create the Life You Really Want," Success Consciousness. Accessed August 3, 2017. http://www.successconsciousness.com/guest_articles/acts-of-courage.htm

Washingtonsblog. "42 Admitted False Flag Attacks," Washingtonsblog. com. February 9, 2015. Accessed September 20, 2017. http://www. washingtonsblog.com/2015/02/41-admitted-false-flag-attacks.html.

Wernerhoff, Carl. "Was Martin Bryant Framed?" The Port Arthur Massacre. Nexus Magazine. Volume 13, Number 4. July 2006. Accessed September 5, 2023, http://www.whale.to/b/wernerhoff.html

WebMD Senior Editorial Staff. "What You Need to Know About Omega-3s," Last updated on November 02, 2016. Accessed April 15, 2017. http://www.webmd.com/diet/ss/slideshow-omega-3-health-benefits.

Whitman, Gren. "OPINION: Oswald: "I'm Just a Patsy" — The JFK Assassination Revisited," Common sense: Straight Talk for the Eastern Shore. Jan 18, 2022. Accessed September 5, 2023, https://www. commonsenseeasternshore.org/opinion-oswald-im-just-a-patsy-the-jfk-assassination-revisited.

Wikihow. "How to Leave an Abusive Relationship," last modified October 30, 2020. http://www.wikihow.com/Leave-an-Abusive-Relationship.

Wikipedia. "Star Wars (film)." Last modified March 13, 2018. https:// en.wikipedia.org/wiki/Star_Wars_(film).

Yates, Douglas. "9/11 was a false-flag event; war was the hidden agenda," Daily News Miner. Last modified September 12, 2017. Accessed May 8, 2018, http://www.newsminer.com/opinion/community_perspectives/ was-a-false-flag-event-war-was-the-hidden-agenda/article_13f614aa-9789-11e7-8277-7b0b994cb144.html.

Zetter, Kim. "April 13, 1953: CIA OKs MK-ULTRA Mind-Control Tests," Wired. April 13 2010. Accessed August 21, 2017. https://www. wired.com/2010/04/0413mk-ultra-authorized/.

About the Author:

Shahryar Sadree is a self-educated serial entrepreneur with over 30 years of knowledge and experience running his own businesses. *Shaun, as he is known by friends and family*, has been working with multi-million dollar-a-year companies as a consultant since 2004. Sadree has written and published 2 other self-improvement books, and works with clients for personal and business development coaching.

Shahryar is a 7th generation Royal, related to **Constantine I**, the **King of Georgia**. He is one of many talented and driven men in his family, to include **Mohammad-Taghi Bahar**, later known as *Malck o-sho' ara Bahar*, and **Haj Sheikh Ahmad Bahar**, both who are noted Persian writers, poets, and politicians.

For more information on this author, or if you are interested in personal coaching, please visit:

Shahryarsadree.com

Review Date: April 2022
Review by: Barbara Bamberger Scott
Verified and provided by: The US Review of Books

"It takes courage to accept change. Courage decimates fear and opens the doorway to freedom."

In a wide-ranging exploration of life's many challenges, self-help author Sadree believes that anyone might sometimes experience the sense of being "down in a hole." His message involves rising up, grasping freedom, and removing walls that limit thinking and keep one from positive actions. According to the author, a total change, requiring great courage, is necessary at times to rise out of the hole. He praises activists like Rosa Parks and Mahatma Gandhi and speaks of "the force" that pervades the movie Star Wars—a force that all of nature, including one's mind, can generate and utilize. He notes that Thomas Edison was told he was "too stupid to learn anything," and Walt Disney lost a job because he "lacked imagination." Beethoven was deaf, and Stevie Wonder was blind. Yet they all rose up and achieved remarkable feats. Sadree advises self-discipline, visualization of outcomes, an understanding and reprogramming of the subconscious mind, and the development of "Smart" goals: "Specific," "Measurable," "Achievable," "Relevant," and "Time Bound."

Sadree, a business and leadership consultant, displays a broad panorama of points to ponder in his book. He describes multiple strategies and presents sources from ancient Greek sages to Ben Franklin, Albert Einstein, and modern-day counselors like Tony Robbins. His approach to the reader is direct and personal, as he recalls his own experiences of "the hole" and suggests that most Americans have felt trapped by the restrictions and implications of Covid. He also cites national, political realities that can evince a sense of demoralization and urges rational steps to control oneself rather than be controlled. Sadree's vital message is aimed at a younger generation that may be quick to give up and an older one that may sometimes experience disillusionment at continuing trends. Both groups will find encouragement and motivation through his solid counsel.

Review Date: April 2022
Review by: Cherie Doyen, Ph.D
Verified and provided by: Proisle Publishing Services LLC

"Shahryar Sadree shares an awakening story that will deliver a remarkable message especially to today's youth."

"Down in a Hole" is a work of art written to talk through how a person thinks and how we will be able to manage our state of mind. It discusses the broad subject of the power of our subconscious mind as well as the levels of the human mind.

This work suggests that the subconscious is our mental database of past observations and conclusions. It stores memories, values, and vocabulary in a connected form, presumably in the depths of our brain. Our subconscious mind holds information from experience or learning. This information can be retrieved from memory and brought into awareness at any time. Whatever we nurture in our subconscious mind will one day become a reality once the mind accepts the idea, execution will follow.

Shahryar "Shaun" Sadree the author, noted that the contents of this book makes what is usually difficult to swallow becomes pretty easy to digest, which are some of the surprises that you will find inside of this book. Most of us can't accept the simplicity of programming the human mind. "Master this amazing tool and you will master your life. The mind is truly the most powerful tool I've discovered yet!"

"Researching and writing this book changed the course of my life. Everything I had learned up to that point was up for questioning... I was living a complete lie. What I found was not only shocking but also very inspiring!"
-Shahryar Sadree

This compelling book is a must-read and to be shared with everyone.

Review Date: April 2022
Review by: Rimaletta Ray, Ph.D
Verified and provided by: Proisle Publishing Services LLC

Shahryar "Shaun" Sadree delivers an awe-inspiring message which aims to uplift the generation of today from a depressive state that relates to being "Down in a hole."

He suggests that the mastery of our subconscious mind is vital to achieving solidarity with our positive outlook in life, as well as our freedom in what we pursue in life. Shaun also delivers his arguments with such relevance that tackles pop culture for ease of relatability. One would be how he reintroduced the concept of "the force"—a Star Wars movie reference—which is a powerful tool that is derived from internal control of mind and nature which originates from sheer 'will' and recognition of one's own strength, binding everything in existence, living and not. Suggesting that we too can manipulate our very nature and environment by wanting it bad enough. But unlike how it is generated in the movie universe, the control of it that we can manage in reality is by employing a cluster of goals that makes up what is generally perceived as smart. But in this case, the author managed to come up with a quirky set of acronyms for ease of retention. In this book, being smart means setting goals that are "Specific," "Measurable," "Achievable," "Relevant" and "Time-Bound". He effectively relates the prominent personalities through generations to the struggles of a common individual such as the juxtaposition of traits from the ideal character and achievements. These juxtapositions further solidify his claim that it is possible and rewarding to control our subconscious minds to achieve great things in life, despite our incapacities which— possibly—can only be rooted in excuse and procrastination.

Sadree also gives gravity to the external factors that influence humanity as a whole, giving light to how vulnerable we are to all kinds of stimulations that manipulate our absolute perspective. With a touch of activism, he supplements the notion that we are constantly under surveillance and control of those who are closer to the origin of currency—or the 0.1% of the population—and how we've come to accept terms with this kind of oppression. With this, he offers us the ultimate solution of taking back the reins for ourselves and lays them all neatly in this book.

Shahryar Sadree, is a Life and Business strategist who derives his lessons through personal encounters in the field. He has a broad experience in consultation for several companies. "Down in a Hole" may be his best piece of self-help literature, but he does offer more by authoring several books that cater to Self-improvement.

Review Date: May 2022
Review by: Dr. Rhonda A. Jaudon
Verified and provided by: Proisle Publishing Services LLC

"Down in A Hole" ventures to a rarely tapped premise of self-help and discovery where internal and individual problems are given light by exposing the flaws of ones thought process and as well as society itself. Here the author "Shahryar 'Shaun' Sadree" tackles the 'Micro' and 'Macro' causes of the problems of a common man which ultimately leads one to sink further into depression, or— in this case—down in a hole.

From an Ill-placed common point of view which prolongs our dilemma, to the "Endgame" which emancipates us from this narrow vision of the world, the contents in this book are purposefully lined-up to help everyone adapt to a state of mind that convinces us that we are in control of how we think, act and live. The best discourse of this book is that; the author—Shaun—argues that it's more than just knowing what is universally right, and what is the correct thing to do that makes us a better version of ourselves, but it also takes self-convincing, discipline and perception, where even we make ourselves believe that what appears to be a 'defeat' is an undeniable win. But it's more than just letting ourselves believe that a 'loss' is a 'win', rather, it's about acting it to be so. "Converting Defeat into a Priceless Asset."

This work heavily leans to "Subconscious Programming" as an ultimate solution. "Sub-consciousness" (or the subconscious mind) in latter studies is a fixed sense or set of behavior that influences our actions in response to stimulations; environmental stimulations. These stimulants can be induced in order to expose certain subconscious actions from unsuspecting subjects, also known as "priming". Also, an existing study known as "Classical Conditioning" comes to relevance as it involves a learning process focused more on involuntary behaviors, using associations with neutral stimuli to evoke a specific involuntary response. But setting all the theories aside, Sadree presents the practice to us in a conveniently straightforward way.

From proven techniques to relatable scenarios, it is all pretty much spoon fed with none left to speculate. **If you are looking for a simplified way to lift yourself from being down, literally, and emotionally, then "Down in A Hole" is exactly what you need to pick up this instant.**

Shahryar Shaun Sadree led an interesting set of careers over the years including business and life coaching and authored 2 other books dedicated to self-help. He also has dedicated himself to research about subjects involving Philosophy, Psychology, Behavioral Sciences, Universal laws, and History.